First Battalion/Sixth Division/Second Company/Third Platoon
(1918)

In honor of Stephen Garrett, the man who demonstrated gentleness.

All rights reserved. No part of this publication may be reproduced, distributed, or transmitted in any form or by any means, including photocopying, recording, or other electronic or mechanical methods, without the prior written permission of the author, except in the case of brief quotations embodied in critical reviews and certain other noncommercial uses permitted by copyright law. For permission requests, contact the author at GammonIrons@gmail.com. ©2018.

Front Cover: Portrait of Corporal Stephen Garrett, 1917.

What is absurd and monstrous about war is that men who have no personal quarrel should be trained to murder one another in cold blood.

Stephen Garrett

INTRODUCTION

THE BIG PICTURE

This is a story which might well have been written to illustrate George Washington's famous words: "The first qualification of a soldier is fortitude under fatigue and privation. Courage is only the second. Hardship, poverty and actual want are the soldier's best school."

It is a story about soldiers, not about war. I attempted to write the most grim and realistic account of what soldiers really experienced from the viewpoint of the American Infantry soldier in the Great War.

Its heroes are the men of a single platoon of a U.S. Infantry Battalion, during the few brief months of 1918 when the rising weight of American manpower on the Western Front broke the back of the Imperial German Army - and paid the price of victory with their blood.

I paid no heed to high strategy. I do tell of famous battles - Belleau Wood, Soissons, Mont Blanc - but scarcely mention them by name. I did not seek to paint on a broader canvas than could be seen by the men with whom I was concerned. Men who were rarely sure where they were going, what was going to happen to them next, or whether on waking they would live to see the sun go down: much less of the names which history would assign to the battles they fought. I entitled this book *"Soldier! Oh, Solider!"* because the hero tells his tale of fellow enlisted men fighting death and becoming wounded in fields, in woods, in muddy ravines, on rocky hillsides, in village streets or in shell-holes waist-deep in water.

Readers will learn what it is like to be pinned down for hours under the pitiless violence of artillery fire, counting the seconds between salvoes, never quite sure if the next one won't be the last one having your name on it. You share the sounds, the sights and above all the smells of the battlefield, of trenches where the stench of decomposing bodies is never absent. You come to understand something of what it means to be always tired, always tormented by lice, always afraid however bold in action and usually hungry. Yet, you will learn how men - quite ordinary men, mostly young, mostly without previous experience of battle though led by a few veterans, acquire the art of endurance, instinctively applying the experience of each hour toward survival through the next.

These men of whom I tell are not of one pattern, but of the wide variety always found in hastily-raised citizen armies. Some are strong, some weak: some after long endurance reach the breaking point; others, seemingly cast in anything but an heroic mold, fight both bravely and skillfully when the iron dice of war roll on the battlefield.

You learn, too, how these young men respond to true leadership. You will be impressed with the tremendous importance of little breaks in the deadly monotony of combat. And occasionally there is a real break - as when a whole truckload of our doughboys take a wrong turn in the darkness as they are moving up to the front. Dawn finds them alone on a hill-road, ending at a village deserted by every living presence except a flock of chickens.

Through it all, the somber shadow of the front remains always in the minds of the men. When there, the constant query is when do we get relieved? Every rumor is seized upon eagerly by the hopeful, discounted by the cynics. When away from the front, every small occurrence is dissected for signs that we may be going back.

Get up and go back they did. No American can read of these men and their doings without feeling enormous pride.

THE BIGGER PICTURE

Who is Stephen Garrett? Born 1895 and died 1992; however, this is not the sum of his life. It is between these two dates that I remember a friend. I first met this gentle man when I was not even in school. I knew him as a neighbor farmer who invited my family over for spring strawberries and autumn peaches. He allowed me to fish and swim in a pond that he, and a single mule with a drag pan, had created. I never knew him but as a kind elderly farmer. Years later, I became a caregiver to Stephen Garrett and it wasn't until then that I learned about his heroic past. I would set for hours and listen to his adventures of the Great War. Once, I mistakenly called it World War I only to be corrected; I learned that this war was the Great War. It was the Great War because so many sacrificed their lives believing that this one war would end all wars and humanity could have a future of liberty and peace!

Stephen Garrett's ancestry was steeped in history. His grandfather (Richard Henry Garrett) owned the small farm in Caroline County, Virginia where John Wilkes Booth was trapped in the Garret barn. The Union soldiers burned the barn and the infamous J.W. Booth was caught. I am honored to bring this story to the attention of those living in America during the 21ST century. May we always be blessed by those who answer the call to liberty and peace, expecting nothing in return but our willingness to carry on the great experiment we call democracy.

Thank you Stephen Garrett!

Gammon Irons

Note to reader: This work is not intended to be an autobiography of Stephen Garrett. This work is the reminiscing of a period of a gentleman's life he lived more than seventy-seven years before its retelling. The author makes no claim of authenticity but has tried to research and validate all the information written to the best of his ability.

Military Command Structure

Sixth Division Commander
    Major General Campbell
First Battalion Commander
    Major Adams
Second Company Commander
    Captain Anderson
Third Platoon Leader
    Lieutenant Harris
    Squad Leaders
        Sergeant Kevin Lark
        Sergeant Fenton Powell
        Sergeant Douglas Walker
        Attack Leaders
            Corporal Oscar Bennett
            Corporal Stephen Garrett
            Corporal Clayton Morrow
            Corporal Kyle Phillips
            Corporal Lucas Turner (Corporal of the Guard)
            Squad Members
                Private Alton Bloomfield
                Private Cornelius Dempsey
                Private Jay Edwards
                Private Felix Franks
                Private Ivan Foster
                Private Ellis Garland
                Private Nelson Green
                Private Harmon Hartman
                Private Edwin Howell
                Private Larry Larkson
                Private Perry Mitchell
                Private Ollie Parker
                Private Dennis Perry
                Private Henry Peterson

Private Reginald Rogers
Private Carroll Sanders
Private Aaron Sullivan
Private Rufus Thompson

Western Front of the Great War

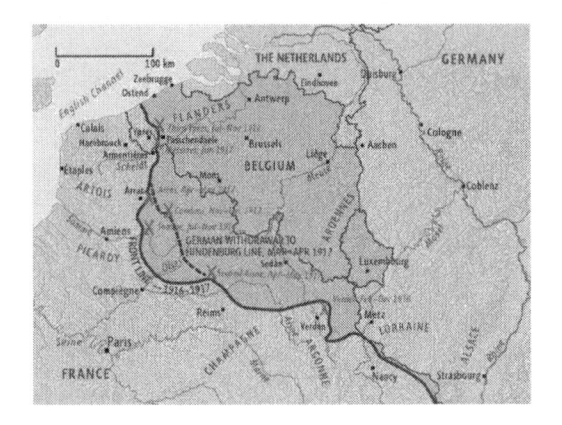

CHAPTER ONE

Dusk, like soft blue smoke, fell with the dying spring air and settled upon the northern French village. In the uncertain light one and two story buildings set along the crooked street showed crisply, bearing a resemblance to false teeth in an ashen-old face. To young Stephen Garrett, disconsolate as he leaned against the outer wall of the French canteen, upon whose smooth white surface his body made an unseemly blot, life was worth little.

For nine interminable months Corporal Garrett had been in France, shunted from one place to another, acting out the odious office of the military police, working as a stevedore beside ill-odored laborers, helping to build cantonments and reservoirs for new soldiers ever arriving from the United States.

And he was supposed to be a soldier. He had enlisted with at least the tacit understanding that he was some day to fight. At the recruiting office in Richmond, Virginia the bespangled sergeant had told him: "Join the army and see some action." And the heart of Stephen Garrett had fled to the rich brogue and campaign ribbons that the sergeant professionally wore.

But was this action? Was this war? Was this for what Stephen Garrett had come to France? Well, he told himself, it was not. Soldiering with a shovel. A hell of a way to treat an American soldier. There were plenty of Frenchmen to dig holes in the ground, but not many of them could qualify as sharpshooters. And Garrett swelled his chest a trifle, noticing the glint of the metal marksmanship badge on his tunic.

Resting beside him on the ground was a display of unopened food tins above which rose the slender necks of bottles. Of the bottles there were four, white wine of the northern French vineyards. Excessive in number were the cans, and they looked as if their contents were edible. But Garrett was not sure. He had bought them from the wizened little French clerk who had regarded him with suspicion through the window of the canteen. For this suspicion, this slight hostility, Garrett did not blame the little Frenchman. He had, he realized, made an ass of himself by pointing to ambiguously labeled cans piled on the shelves inside the canteen and saying: "la combien?"[1] Now he possessed a choice array of cans of whose contents he knew nothing. All that he asked was that he might be able to eat it.

That morning he had marched into the town with his tired platoon from a small deserted railway station some miles distant. Once assigned to the houses in which they were to be billeted, the men had unstrapped their blankets and fallen asleep. But not Garrett. He had explored the village with an eye to disposing of the mass of soiled and torn franc-notes which he carried in his pocket. In the French canteen he had found the place for which he was looking. And so he had stood before the clerk, demanding to buy as much of the stock as he could carry.

But the clerk had closed the window, leaving Garrett with a handful of French money and the tinned food and four bottles of vin blanc. Hence his disconsolation. The roll of paper felt unnatural, superfluous in his pocket. He was tempted to fling it away. In the morning the platoon would find the canteen and buy the last can, the last bottle.

Restive, he ran his lean fingers through his uncombed hair, wondering vaguely whether it were true that his regiment was soon to depart for the front.

---

[1] How much?
[2] An irreverent term for anyone of French heritage.
[3] A French term for cheap red wine.
[4] A wound garnered from the Spanish-American war.

It must be true, he decided. There had been an untoward attitude on the part of his officers since the moment that the departure of the platoon had been made known. Their destination had been scrupulously kept from them. In corroboration, a long-range gun boomed sullenly in the distance.

The noise produced in him a not unpleasant shiver of apprehension. He met it, summoning a quiet smile of scorn. Yes, he would be glad to go to the front, to that vague place from which men returned with their mutilated bodies. Not that he was vengeful. His feeling for the German army was desultory, a blend of kaleidoscopic emotions in which hate never entered. But in conflict, he felt, would arise a reason for his now unbearable existence.

The grinning weakness which men call authority had followed him since the day of his enlistment at the beginning of the war. It had turned thoughts of valor into horrible nightmares, the splendor of achievement into debased bickering. Most of the men, it seemed to him, had not entered the army to further the accomplishment of a common motive; they had enlisted or had been made officers and gentlemen - Congress had generously made itself the cultural father of officers - for the purpose of aiding their personal ambitions.

It had darkened. Garrett gathered up his sorry feast and sauntered off through the shaking, mysterious shadows to his pallet of straw.

Stretched out upon individual beds of straw which had been strewn over the stone floor, the members of the platoon were lying before a huge fireplace that drew badly in the early spring wind. In all of their nine months in France this was the first time that they had thus lain, not knowing what was to come on the following day, nor caring, being only satisfied by the little warmth which came from the fireplace, by their sense of feeling intact and comfortable.

Garrett sighed, elongating his limbs beneath his blanket. He made an effort to rise, and succeeded in resting the weight of his torso on his arm which he had crooked under him. Cautiously he felt for a cigarette beneath his tunic, which he was using for a pillow. He got the cigarette and a match, then held them in his hand, hesitant.

His eyes, large and dolorous, searched the dimly lit room, scanning the recumbent figures to discover whether they were asleep. Men were lying, their shoes beside their heads, their army packs, rifles, leaning against the wall and the remainder of their equipment scattered nearby. The men were silent, motionless.

"I guess I can risk it," thought Garrett, and he carefully struck the match and lit his cigarette.

As the match was rubbed over the floor, heads appeared; the stillness was broken.

Clayton Morrow, the Mississippi gambler, with his everlasting dice-throwing, which every payday that the platoon had thus far known had won for him more money than his company commander received from the United States Government.

"Oh," Morrow thought, "you have another cigarette."

"You got fifty francs off me last month. I think you ought to give me a smoke!" The voice was reproachful.

Effectually and instantly Morrow checked the avalanche of reproach: "Hey, you fellas, there's beaucoup mail up at regimental headquarters."

The clumsy shadows in the darkened room answered: "Aw bunk."

"Cut out that crap."

"How do you get this way, Morrow? You know there ain't no mail up at regimental."

"Well," Morrow sighed, "if you all don' wanna heah f'm your mammy I don' give a damn. . . . Oh-o. What you all got, Garrett?"

Garrett had arrived at his billet, his arms filled with the bottles of wine and the cans of the questionable contents.

Candles were lit and set on the helmets of the men. Bodies rose to a sitting posture, eyes on Garrett.

"Gimme a drink, Garrett!"

"Hooray, look what Garrett's got."

"Yeh, gimme a drink."

The voices were clamorous.

"Gimme, gimme? Was your mouth bored out with a gimlet," Garrett jeered. "Why didn't you buy some?"

They formed a semi-circle around the fireplace in front of which Garrett sat with his plunder.

Over the bottles they grew noisily talkative.

"Say, have you fellows seen any of these new guys here?" asked Garrett. "I was walkin' down one of the streets by the Frog[2] canteen and one of 'em asked me if I was in the balloon corps. I told him yes,

---

[2] An irreverent term for anyone of French heritage.

and asked him how he guessed it, and he said, 'Oh, I saw that balloon on your cap.'"

"They sure are a bunch of funny birds. I ask one of 'em how long he'd been over on this side and he said: 'About three weeks - seen anybody that's come over lately?'"

A contingent of soldiers that had arrived in the village that afternoon were, therefore, objects of scorn and hostility.

"Aw, they're some of them fellahs that the wind blew in. Pretty soon they'll have the home guards over here."

"They will like hell! If you could get them home guards away from home they'd sure have to hump. They're home guards - they guard our women while we're over here." The speaker seemed afraid that his listeners would not understand that he was stressing the word home.

"Yeh, they's one of 'em guardin' my gal too close. I got a lettah . . ."

"You're lucky to get any kind of a letter. Here I been for three months and not a word. I don't know whether they all forgot about me or what," Garrett ended gloomily.

"Aw cheer up, Garrett, old boy. Maybe your mail was on that transport that got sunk."

A head was thrust in the door. It was the Sergeant. "Pipe down, you damned recruits. Lights are supposed to be out at eight o'clock. If you guys want to get work detail for the rest of your lives . . ."

"All right, you dirty German spy. Get the hell out of here and let us sleep."

All of the candles had been put out as soon as the voice of the Sergeant was heard. The men had flung themselves on their beds. Now each one pretended to be asleep.

"Who said that?" The Sergeant was furious. "I'll work you birds till your shoes fall off."

The room answered with loud and affected snores. The Sergeant, in all of his fierceness, disappeared.

CHAPTER TWO

It was morning.

Sergeant Douglas Walker, bearing with proud satisfaction the learning and culture he had acquired in the course of three years at a small Middle-Western university, walked down the Rue de Dieu in a manner which carried the suggestion that he had forgotten the belt of his breeches.

Approaching a white two-story stone building which age and an occasional long-distance German shell had given an air of solemn decrepitude, Sergeant Walker unbent enough to shout stiltedly: "Mail Call! Mail Call!"

His reiterated announcement was unnecessary. Already half-dressed soldiers were rushing through the entrance of the building and toward the approaching Sergeant.

"All right, you men. If you can't appear in uniform, get off of the company street." Sergeant Walker was commanding.

In their eagerness to hear the list of names called out the men forgot even to grumble, but scrambled back through the doorway overflowing the long-hall off of which were six rooms, devoid of furniture, which had been converted into barracks.

Sergeant Walker, feeling the entire amount of pleasure to be had from the added importance of distributing the mail - the first the platoon had received in two months - cleared his throat, took a steadfast position and gave his attention to the small bundle of letters which he held in his hand.

He deftly riffled them twice without speaking. Then he separated the letters belonging to the non-commissioned officers, the corporals, and sergeants from those addressed to the privates. The non-commissioned officers received their letters first.

At last: "Corporal Garrett," Walker read off.

"Here, here I am. Back here." Corporal Garrett was all aflutter. Separated from the letter by a crowd of men, he stood on tiptoe and reached his arm far over the shoulder of the man in front of him.

"Pass it back to him? Pass it back to him?" voices impatiently asked.

"No!" Sergeant Walker was a commander, every inch of him. "Come up and get it, Garrett."

"Hey, snap out of it, will ya! Call off the rest of the names."

A path was made, and Garrett finally received the letter.

Walker looked up. "If you men don't shut up, you will never get your mail!"

"Corporal Morrow!"

"Hee-ah. Gimme that lettah. That's fm mah sweet mammah." Morrow wormed his small, skinny body through the men, fretfully calling at those who did not make way quickly enough. He grasped the letter. Then he started back, putting the letter in his pocket unopened.

"Poor old Morrow. Gets a letter and he can't read."

"Ain't that a waste of stationery?"

"Why don't you ask the captain to write an' tell your folks not to send you any more mail? Look at all the trouble you cause these mail clerks."

Several men offered to read the letter to Morrow, but he did not answer.

An hour later the Sergeant was walking up and down in front of the billets, blowing his whistle.

"Shake it up, you men. Don't you know you're supposed to be ready for drill at nine o'clock?"

"Drill! I thought we come up here to fight," voices grumbled, muttering obscene phrases directed at General Pershing, the Company Commander, and the Sergeant.

Men scurried out of their billets, struggling to get on their packs and to fall in line before the roll was called.

"Fall in!" the Sergeant shouted, standing before the platoon. "Right dress!" he commanded sharply and ran to the right of the platoon, from where he told one man to draw in his waist and another to move his feet, and so on, until he was satisfied that the line was reasonably straight. "Steady, front!" And in a very military manner he placed himself in the proper place before the company and began to call the roll.

"All present or accounted for, sir," he reported to the Captain, a note of pride and of a great deed nobly done ringing in his voice.

The Sergeants fell back in rear of their platoons and the Commander ordered "squads right." The hob-nailed boots of the men on the cobblestones echoed hollowly down the street.

Stupid-looking old Frenchmen, a few thick-waisted women, and a scattering of ragged children dully watched the company march down the street. For the most part they were living in the advance area because they had no other place to go and because they feared to leave the only homes that they had ever known.

The platoon marched out of the town along a gravel road and into a green, evenly plotted field, where they were deployed and where, to their surprise, a number of sacks, filled with straw, had been hung from a row of scaffolding.

The platoon faced the sacks, were maneuvered so that each man would be standing in front of one of the dummies and were ordered to fix bayonets. Sergeant Walker, the nostrils of his stubby nose flaring wide with zeal, began his instructions.

"All right, you men. Now you want to forget that these are sacks of straw. They are not at all. They are dirty Huns - Huns that raped the Belgians, Huns that would have come over to the good old U. S.A. and raped our women if we hadn't got into the war. Now, men, I want to see some action, I want to see some hate when you stick these dirty Huns. I want to see how hard you can grunt."

"All ready now. Straight thrust. One, two, three — now!"

As a body the platoon lunged their bayonets into the cloth-covered straw.

"Great, God! Is that all the pep you've got? Why, you men are stale. What the hell did you come over here to fight for? Did you ever hear that you were supposed to be saving the world for democracy? Now, try it again, and put some punch in it this time. Let's hear your grunt."

The action was repeated. "Rotten!" yelled the Sergeant. "What the hell are you going to do when you get up to the front? Do you think this is an afternoon tea? You act like a bunch of ribbon-counter clerks, and that's what I believe most of you are. Now let's try the butt stroke."

"Butt stroke. One, two, three – now! Oh, hell. Where are you aiming, Thompson? Remember, you've missed him with the bayonet and you're trying to sock him in the crotch - in the crotch, mind you, with the butt of your rifle."

Several of the men caught the frenzy of the Sergeant, and at each command they ran, gritting and grinding their teeth, and grunted at the pieces of straw. From the terrific onslaught one of the dummies was severed from the scaffold, and the Sergeant cried out: "That's the first real spirit I've seen today. That's the way to kill them!" he called to the man who had wrested the dummy from its place. "Come up here and show these dopes how to kill."

Exultant, the man left his place and strutted over to the Sergeant. Taking a position before one of the dummies, he proceeded to show the rest of the platoon how really and frightfully to stab the dummies until their stuffing broke through the sacks.

"He's working to be a Sergeant, the dirty scut. And oh, if he does get to be a three-striper won't he make us step around. Boy!" Garrett muttered to Morrow, who was standing next to him and whose bayonet had failed even to pierce the covering of the sack.

"He won't pull none of that old stuff on me. Ah'll tell Lieutenant Harris and he'll make him be good or I won't give him any more money to gamble with," Morrow drawled.

"You sure have got a stand-in with Harris, Morrow. I often wondered how you did it."

"Hell, that's easy. When he was down at St. Nazaire, I lent him 'bout a thousand francs to gamble with, and he ain't never paid me."

The platoon assembled and marched back to their billets.

CHAPTER THREE

Three days were spent by the platoon at the little village. On the evening of the third day, just as the men had formed in a long, impatient line before the field kitchen, with their aluminum food receptacles held out to catch the thin, reddish stew surly thrown at them, the Company Commander walked among them bearing words of dour import. Captain Anderson talked softly and gently, wringing the words from his heart, burnishing them with a note of sadness: "Stay close to your billets tonight after chow, men. We're moving up to the front sometime tonight."

He passed by them, and those whom he passed shuffled their feet, looking furtively at the ground. There was little comment. The shuffling line was a funereal. Men smiled at Captain Anderson, but their smiles lacked certitude.

When they had packed their belongings in the stipulated military manner the pall remained, vaguely hanging over them, drawing them together in their common aversion from the future. In the rooms they sat on their packs, nervously waiting to move.

The moonlight streamed in through the window and showed the gray whitewashed walls of the deserted room. The fireplace was a black maw.

Night fell in mysterious folds, giving the appearance of unfamiliarity to the squat French houses, the spired Gothic church, the trees which drooped their boughs in a stately canopy over the smooth gray road.

The men, their feet striking against the cobblestones, clumped through the village streets and along the road.

The sector toward which the platoon was moving had once been the scene of violent conflict, but of late, with the more important military maneuvers taking place farther west, it had dropped into a peaceful desuetude. It lay a few miles from Verdun, among the green-covered concealed fortresses, from which the noses of mammoth artillery unexpectedly rose. Tops of thickly wooded hills reared evenly in an unbroken line. Between the crests the shadow-hidden valleys rested serene, content with their secrets of the dead. Along the base of the mauve chain of hills wound a trench from which French soldiers, most of whom were on the farther side of fifty, sat around in dugouts and drank their rations of pinard[3] or squatted, their shirts off, hunting lice in the seams.

The platoon marched up in the pitch-black night, slipping, from time to time, off the slimy duckboards which had been placed in the bottom of the trench to prevent traffic from being buried in the mud. Their packs, with hip rubber boots, bandoliers of ammunition, bombs, and shovels, bowed them over as they cautiously and cursingly made their way through the communication trench.

Somewhere ahead a white light flared with a sputtering noise.

"Stand fast!" Lieutenant Harris called out peremptorily.

The men stood as rocks, their arms crooked, covering their faces. The light dropped slowly and unemotionally to the ground, dying out. Again, all was blackness.

Sergeant Walker, who had gone ahead as billeting officer, now joined the platoon and piloted the men into the trench. The main trench was

---

[3] A French term for cheap red wine.

much wider than the communication trench, but passage along it was difficult because of the half-checkered manner in which it had been laid out.

Not waiting to be relieved, the French soldiers one by one had disappeared into the night. Now the platoon stood silent and ill at ease. No one knew where to go, and so the entire body was ordered to remain standing in the firing bays until morning.

Dawn broke upon a desolate field where rusty barbed wire clung awkwardly to the posts on which it had been strung. There were a few gnarled and stunted trees, the wreck of what once had been a French farmhouse, and that was all. Garrett peered over the parapet, wondering how near he was to the enemy. He stepped upon the firing step of firm clay. A few yards away were the torn and rusted tracks of the Paris-Metz railway. Beyond that was just an uncared for field, which, in the distance, lost itself in the gray of the horizon.

He experienced a strange feeling of awe, as if he were looking upon another world. The early sun threw the trees and barbed wire into a queer perspective and gave them a harsh, unreal aspect.

In the early springtime this particular sector looked very much like one of the calm farms which Garrett was accustomed to see in many parts of Virginia. The birds sang as lightheartedly, the sun was as bright, the grass was as green and fragrant over the slightly rolling field. All was quite as it should be. Only Garrett was out of the picture. Ordinarily he would have been contemplating such a pastoral scene from the window of a railway train or from a mid-Atlantic farmhouse, where he would have been spending his summer vacation. He would have been dressed in a blue flannel suit, with a straw sailor hat, a white shirt of some soft summery material and a rather striking tie. His hose would have been of silk and his cool white underclothes would have been of the athletic type, Garrett mused.

Then he became aware of himself. In place of the straw sailor hat there lay very heavily on his head a steel helmet that, though he had thought it chic for a while, was now no more distinguished-looking than the aluminum dish in which his food was rationed to him. He had worn his drab shirt for two weeks, and there were black rings around the collar and wrists. His gas-mask, girded over his chest, looked foul and unclean; he had used it for a pillow, for a dining-table, and often, he realized, it had been thrown in some muddy place when he had sickened of having it about him like the ever-present ancient mariner's albatross. The knees of his breeches were as soiled and as uncomfortable as his shirt, and his puttees and shoes were crusted thickly with dried mud.

His stock-taking of his dress was interrupted by the knowledge that a persistent vermin was exploring the vicinity of his upper body. He could not apprehend it because of his gas-mask, which, suspended from his neck, was strapped to his chest.

After the first few days life in the trenches became inordinately dull, so dull that an occasional shell fired from the artillery of either side was a signal for the members of the platoon to step into the trench and speculate where it struck.

Every night two squads of the platoon stood watch while the others slept. Garrett, with Perry, was stationed in a shell hole a few yards ahead of the front line. The shell hole was half-filled with water and it was cold. After three or four hours the hip rubber boots made Garrett think that his feet were a pair of dead fish in a refrigerator.

It was customary for the Corporal of the Guard and the Lieutenant each night to inspect the outposts, but because the ground was wet and because of the strands of unmanageable barbed wire the Lieutenant had stayed in his dugout, permitting the Corporal of the Guard to have the honor of inspecting.

One night, when the dampness seemed like a heavily draped ghost that wanted to kiss Garrett's entire body, and when his eyes had completely tired from the strain of imagining that the stumps and posts in the field were moving, Garrett fell asleep. In his cramped position, sitting on a board over a shell hole, with his feet in the icy water, Garrett's sleep was full of fantastic dreams. He might have slept until the noonday sun awakened him, had he not slipped from his seat and sprawled into the water. This awakened Perry, who invariably went back to sleep, remaining so until the watch was over.

"What the hell's coming off?" Garrett awakened with a jerk. "Christ, it's time to go in."

They observed the sun, which spread out rays of silvery light before it as it slowly rose. The sky was almost smoked-pearl colored, and before it the trees and barbed wire made sharp sentinels.

Silently they picked up their rifles and slunk into the trench. Answering the guards challenging "Halt, who's there?" with an "Oh, shut up," they stepped on the slippery duckboard.

"Say, Garrett, you'd better look out. What the hell were you guys up to last night?" the guard asked.

"What do you mean? We weren't up to anything."

"Well, old Turner came back here after being out to your hole, a-cussin' like hell. He said you guys couldn't take advantage of your friendship with him like that and get away with it."

"I don't know what he meant. Let's beat it, Perry."

They went to their dugout, where they slept with their shoes beneath their heads, to keep, as Garrett almost truthfully remarked, the rats from carrying them away.

The Major's orderly, his dignity wrestling with the slippery footing of the duckboards, marched down the trench from Battalion Headquarters. Stopping in front of the dugout which Garrett and Perry had entered, he removed his helmet, patted his hair, and called: "Is Corporal Garrett in there? Tell Corporal Garrett, Major Adams wants to see him."

His hair a rat's nest, and a heavy beard on his muddy-looking face, Garrett looked out of the entrance of the dugout.

"What's the matter?"

Without answering, the orderly turned about and marched back toward Battalion Headquarters. Garrett followed him.

Major Adams belonged to that type of officer each of which you meet with the feeling that he is the sole survivor of the school of regular soldiers. He was a tall, slim, very erect person. His face was ascetic, though gossip about his personal affairs proclaimed him to be fiercely lustful. He wore his campaign hat adeptly. He limped as he walked, from an unhealed gunshot wound received in the Philippines.[4] Campaign ribbons were strung across his breast. With him authority was as impersonal as the fourth dimension. He was adored and held in awe by half of the battalion.

Corporal Garrett stepped inside the Major's dugout and saluted.

"You wanted to see me, sir?"

"Garrett, you were reported this morning to have gone to sleep while on outpost duty."

---

[4] A wound garnered from the Spanish-American war.

Garrett started visibly. "That's true, sir."

"Well, what the hell kind of a soldier are you, anyway?" Major Adams fairly bit his words loose.

"I don't know, sir. I mean, I guess I've been a pretty good soldier."

"You have like hell, Garrett, and you know it. Now, why did you go to sleep on watch?"

Garrett knew that if he were court-martialed his sentence might be life imprisonment. It might be anything, he reflected, that the group of morons sitting in solemn judgment might decide to give him.

Major Adams also knew it.

"Sir, the hours are too long. Nobody can stay awake when he goes on watch eight hours every night."

"Yes?" Major Adams raised an eyebrow forbiddingly.

"Well, sir, there's two feet of water in the shell hole where my post is, and I guess I got so numb with cold that I went to sleep."

"And you never thought to bail it out? I knew that officers were so damned dumb that they needed dog-robbers,[5] but I didn't know that enlisted men were. Now, Garrett, you haven't a case at all. But" - he was silent a moment -"someday you might make a good soldier. You wouldn't have a chance if you were to get a general court martial, because the judges would have you hung as an example," he said, "I'm going to let this drop. You may go."

---

[5] A soldier that makes problems disappear by whatever means necessary.

Mumbling a "Thank you, sir," Garrett properly about-faced and left the dugout.

CHAPTER FOUR

The platoon had been in the trenches for six weeks. Everything had been quiet, well-ordered. Occasionally a shell from the German batteries would start lazily off and end up with terrific speed in the platoon's trench. Once or twice men were killed when the shells struck, and their bodies were hurried away to the dressing station. One morning the body of a red-haired German, an immense fellow with a broad forehead, large wide eyes, and a huge mouth, was found fastened to the strands of barbed wire in front of Garrett's post. There was a hole in his side made by the explosion of a small hand-bomb. Besides that, there was nothing of interest.

In fact, there was too little of interest. Not even a prisoner had been taken, although the Colonel of the regiment had let it be known that the first man to capture a prisoner would be given a fifteen-days leave to Aix-le-Bains. So, it was decided that a raiding party was what was needed to resuscitate the platoon from its lethargy.

It was for this reason that when Garrett and Perry set out through the trench toward their shell hole one night they were stopped by the Lieutenant and told that they had been relieved for the night and were to return to their dugout and await his orders.

Garrett was disturbed. He felt as if the Lieutenant's orders had in some way to do with his sleeping on watch. He had not minded the consequences so much when he was walking toward Battalion Headquarters, but now that everything with regard to the affair seemed to have been smoldering, he was fearful. Being rather reckless, probably the first time that Major Adams' remark that he might get a general court martial was fully realized by him was at the moment when he and Perry had been sent back to their dugout.

Now he sat, his head bowed and his hands clasped before him. What the hell was he to do? It was the first time he had thought of his family. What would Katie[6] say when she discovered that he, Stephen Garrett, was in Fort Leavenworth? What would the neighbors say? And his mother? Maybe they might order him to be shot! This was a mess. But no, wasn't there a general order recently made to the effect that no one in the American Expeditionary Forces could be executed without permission of President Wilson? Sure there was.

Good of the old horse-face[7] to think of that. But maybe there was a way to get out of it yet. He considered for a moment the advisability of clambering over the trench and setting forth into that unexplored field, never to return unless he brought a German prisoner with him. Let's see, how had they done it, he mused. There were plenty of heroes who could. They'd just fill their pockets with hand-grenades and blow up a machine-gun nest. "Major Adams, I fulfilled your prediction! Here!" - indicating three fierce-looking Germans with the stump of his left arm, which had been shot off during his single-handed assault. "And there were five more, but I would have had to carry them."

"All right, Garrett and Perry. Are you all set?" Lieutenant Harris, with his aggressive little mustache, was peering into the dugout from the trench. "Here's some blacking for your bayonets. We're going on a raiding party tonight."

"Hooray. That's the stuff." But the voice of Perry was weak and shaky. "When do we go?"

---

[6] Stephen Garrett's fiancé, who later became his life-long wife.
[7] An irreverent slang for President Wilson.

Garrett was nonplussed. He hastily wondered whether he had said a prayer that had been answered. He wanted some source to lay this bit of good fortune to. And at the same time he doubted whether it was unalloyed fortune, whether there was not some disagreeable part to be performed. So he said nothing, but began in a businesslike manner to dim the luster of his bayonet with the blacking Harris had given to him.

"We'll be ready to start in a half-hour. We've got to wait for guides from the Intelligence Section." Lieutenant Harris walked away.

When the guides arrived and the representatives from each platoon were assembled it was night, and so dark that one could not see another in front of him, A Lieutenant and a Sergeant from the Intelligence Section led the way, with Garrett and Perry sandwiched in the middle of the long line that kept from separating by the man in rear holding to the shoulder of the man in front of him.

Instead of leaving the trench by Garrett's shell hole, the party turned in the opposite direction, and, after splashing along the water-covered duckboards for ten or more minutes, climbed over a firing bay and worked their way through a path that a succession of well-placed shells had blown in the barbed wire.

Their feet, scuffing through the tall grass, hissed like a scythe cutting heavy weeds. That, and an occasional cough, were the only noises of the night. Suddenly Garrett's foot struck a large, yielding substance. He felt with his feet, prodding into the thing, which caused a fearful stench to rise.

"Hey, what's this?" he softly called, and the Intelligence Section Sergeant came running back only to exclaim in a voice that had been hardened by one other raiding party: "That? Why, that's only a dead Boche."[8]

A moment afterward an automatic rifle broke nervously into a series of put-put-puts.

As one man, the party fell flat on their stomachs.

"Put-put-put. Put-put-put," cried the automatic rifle.

"Damnation," Harris cursed. "It's somebody from our lines firing at us."

"Well, don't talk so loud," one of the men said angrily, "or you'll have both sides on us."

The Lieutenant from the Intelligence Section gave orders for the men to lie prone and to crawl after him. After a while he rose, motioning for the others to get up.

"I think," he said, talking to Harris in an undertone, "that this is the place where we get back in the trench. Let's count up our men and see if they are all here."

They counted as many times as a surgeon counts the sponges he uses in an operation, but each count only made more certain that there was one man missing. Investigation showed them that the lost man was Private Mitchell, from the adjoining company.

While they were debating upon what course to take, they noticed from their lines a green rocket fired into the air.

"Gas," hoarsely cried the Lieutenant of the Intelligence Section, struggling to get on his respirator.

---

[8] An offensive term for one of German heritage.

Poor Garrett knew not what to do. Before the rocket had been fired, he had about decided to return to look for the missing Private. But with a respirator on he could hardly breathe, not to consider finding his way in the dark. Then of a sudden he whipped off his mask and started off in the direction from which they had crawled. No one noticed his leaving, for each man was too much taken up with his own affairs.

Garrett walked for a while, until he believed he was near the place where the automatic rifle had begun firing at them. He dropped upon his knees, and with his hands spread out as far along the ground as he could stretch them, groped for the lost body. Perspiration was drenching him. It ran down his face and dropped off his chin, to splash unconcernedly on the canvas covering of his mask. He felt as if all the blood of his body was in the veins of his face. There! Certainly, it was a body.

"Mitchell," he whispered. "Mitchell." But there was no answer. He felt along the body until his hand touched the face. It was warm, and then he knew that he had found Mitchell. But not Mitchell! Just a body that had once been Mitchell. For Mitchell was dead. Along the tunic and under the respirator box was a warm, sticky substance. Garrett placed his hand over the breast above the heart. It failed to beat.

"Oh, hell!" he muttered, and started to crawl back, hardly caring whether he reached the raiding party or not.

To have saved Private Mitchell, to have brought him into the trench, staggering under the weight over his shoulder, would, he was aware, have exonerated him completely in the eyes of Major Adams. Further, he would have received either a Distinguished Service Cross or a Croix de Guerre. But how could he, what sort of a fool would he have looked like, carrying a dead man over his shoulder all the way into the trench!

Well, it was simply a case of misplaced heroism. He shrugged his shoulder and went on.

When he arrived at the place where he had left the party, just enough light had broken to enable him to see them sprawled on the ground. With their respirators still on they seemed, in the dimness, like pompous owls.

Garrett approached, casually inquiring why they had not taken off their masks. The Lieutenant of the Intelligence Section, after wildly motioning with his hands, took off his mask, sniffed, and proceeded to curse Garrett for not informing him earlier that the gas had blown away.

"We might have been killed out here any minute, you damned bonehead."

"Yes, and we probably will be killed now if we don't get out of this pretty soon. In five minutes it will be broad daylight. Besides, the gas alarm was all a fake," Garrett answered.

Now all the men had returned their respirators to the boxes, which were fastened by a cord around their necks to their breasts. The Sergeant of the Intelligence Section set out to find the path in the barbed wire, but there was none where he looked. He turned back, the men following after him like lost sheep, and after sneaking along the wire for some minutes, stopped.

"Hey, you over there in the trench. Pass the word along that the raiding party's coming in," the Sergeant of the Intelligence Section called.

One of the sentries in the firing bay heard him, obeyed, and the raiding party dashed through the wire and spilled into the trench. The Company Commander, a former professor of English at a Texas college, emerged from a nearby dugout and warmly wrung the hand of the Lieutenant from the Intelligence section.

"My God, I thought you boys would surely be killed! You see, I - I must have forgotten that the raiding party was still out, and when I heard that machine-gun firing I thought the Germans were making an attack, so I signaled for a barrage."

"But you sent up the gas signal instead of the barrage signal," Harris sourly interposed.

"Yes, that was just it. I thought that I was firing a red rocket and instead I was firing a green one." He broke off quickly. "But you got in all right?"

"All right but for one man," said Harris.

"And where is he?" the Captain asked.

"He - he's dead," Garrett told the assembly.

Harris turned quickly. "Garrett, how do you know he's dead?"

"Well, I saw him. You can see for yourself. He's out there dead."

CHAPTER FIVE

The platoon had been promised a relief for three weeks. Each day some orderly or other would come past, announcing that on the following night there was certain to be a relief. Sometimes, it was the French who once more were to take over the sector. Again, it was the British. British soldiers were reported to have been seen in a nearby town. And the platoon? First it was going to Zeebrugge to storm the Mole. Another time the platoon was to be disorganized and returned to the United States to be used as recruiting and training officers. Sometimes they were all to go on board ship as a mark of appreciation of their valor. This last always was circulated about by one of the older men who had seen service on the battleships.

But one night, before dark, Lieutenant Harris passed the word along that the men were to standby, for the relief was surely coming. And in an hour's time their entire equipment had been assembled, and they stood ready to depart.

Slowly the hours passed, and about midnight the heel of the feet of heavily laden men, their curses and their comment to one another could be heard along the communication trench. Harris, much excited, cautioned each man on sentry duty to look sharply, for it was during the time of relief that the enemy often chose to attack. Finally each of the old sentries had given his special orders to the new sentry, and had slung on his pack and assembled where the platoon stood waiting. They plodded off, sloshing through the communication trench, with now and again a man slipping off the duckboards and floundering hip-deep in the mud. The ditch was tortuous and long. It was morning before the last man had got out and upon the road that took them on their way.

The moon was full and round. Through the shapely leaves of the trees, set at regular intervals along the winding gravel road, it shone, divinely lighting up the way for the tired, mud-caked platoon that straggled along out and away from the front. For the first three miles the platoon had kept intact, but now, one-by-one, the weaker were dropping out to rest by the side of the road. Lieutenant Harris and Sergeant Walker, whose heavy marching equipment had been thrown on the company supply cart, marched gaily in front. There were no packs on their backs to bring their shoulder-blades together until they nearly touched; nor were there any straps to cut into the muscles of their shoulders until their arms were numb.

Finally Garrett, with a nervous, infuriated, impotent "Oh, the hell with it," dropped out and threw his equipment into the ditch. "Let the dirty dogs walk their heads off." Two others dropped out with him and, contrary to orders, all three lit cigarettes.

Puffing away at his cigarette, one of the men began: "If I ever get out of this man's war they'll have to hunt me with cannons to get me in another."

"You tell 'em. They sure will. When I git out of this outfit I'm goin' up into Montana and buy a ranch, and I'm goin' to dig trenches and put up barbed wire and git me some guns and spit at the whole bunch of 'em."

"Why the hell do that? You can do all of that stuff here."

"Yeh, but I wouldn't have no God-damned mail-order shavetails[9] tellin' me what to do and what not to do. That's what I hate."

---

[9] A newly commissioned officer.

"Well, there won't be any more wars after this one, anyway. This is the war to end war. After we lick these Boches everything will be all right."

Garrett rose, faintly nauseated. He flung his cigarette away, threw his equipment over his shoulders, and walked on.

When he arrived at the place where the platoon was to rest he felt quite giddy. He slipped his pack from his shoulders and leaned it against the side of the long, low, slatted bunk house. Of course there was a place there for him to sleep; but, somehow, he did not want to sleep. His stomach seemed about to tie itself into a knot, and he felt that this could be prevented by something hot to drink. He wondered where the galley was; the cooks were sure to have some hot coffee. A man passed, and Garrett asked him whether the cook wagons had yet arrived.

"No, they haven't. They never get here, you know. But there's an old-goat in that building over there that's got some chocolate. Why don't you get some?"

Garrett started away in the direction the man had pointed. Sure enough, the place was crowded with soldiers, and many of them were drinking from thick mugs. Garrett edged toward the counter and asked for a drink. The Y.M.C.A. man filled a mug with hot, thin chocolate. It was the most pleasant sight Garrett had seen in months. He reached for it and was about to drink when something in the man's eyes made him hesitate.

"Well, we don't give this chocolate away!" said the man, turning up a corner of his long, sallow face.

"How much is it?"

"It's half a franc, that's what it is."

Garrett was about to put down the mug of chocolate, when a soldier from the First Regular division stepped forward and offered him the money, and then faced the man behind the counter.

"You're a fine dirty slacker, you are. These men have been out in the trenches for heaven knows how long, and they come back dog-tired and hungry, and you refuse to give them a glass of your skimmed chocolate."

"Oh, never mind," said Garrett. "You know the kind he is. Why talk to him?"

He went back to the bunk house, found his bed, and crawled into it, not stopping to undress.

For five hours the platoon had slept. When dawn, like a fifty-year-old virgin, was showing its hard, cold face, the men had stumbled down into the valley of Bois La Vec. After waiting outside for half an hour they were permitted to enter one of the long, low, vermin-infested bunk houses which lay in the valley. From their sleepless nights on sentry duty, their lack of food, and the long, punishing march from the trenches, they were thoroughly exhausted. Many of the men were in such a state of fatigue that they dropped on the straw beds which had been provided for the French army in 1914, without stopping to take off their muddy shoes. And they slept dreamlessly, sodden beings with senses so dulled they could not think of food. The Mess Sergeant had passed through the bunk house, loudly and virtuously asserting that the daily fare was to be had. Not one of the men had stirred.

A large touring-car, its wind-shield placarded with two white stars cut in a field of red, drove down the valley along the gravel road, and turned toward the bunk houses where the soldiers who preferred sleep to food - and they had not tasted of food for twenty-four hours - were lying.

The motor stopped, and a Lieutenant with a curled mustache, leaned a trifle forward from his seat beside the chauffeur and called: "Where is the sentry of this camp?"

There was no answer.

The Lieutenant stepped out of the car and strode precisely and firmly toward the bunk house.

He spoke loudly. "Where is the sentry of this camp?'

Most of the men were too sleepy even to curse at the intruder. One or two voices impolitely commanded him to "shut up," and one voice mumbled: "Where do you think you're at, anyway?"

Enraged at this disrespect, the Lieutenant decided not to leave until he had aroused someone.

Sergeant Walker, who for once had been forced to sleep with the common soldiers, awakened, and seeing the Lieutenant with the insignia upon his collar worn by officers attached to the General Staff, dove from his bunk like a jack-rabbit, saluting before his feet touched the ground.

The Lieutenant roared: "Where is your company commander?"

"I'll get him, sir!" And Sergeant Walker scurried off.

He returned three feet in rear and three inches to the left of Captain Anderson.

"How do you do, Lieutenant?" Captain Anderson rubbed his sleepy eyes.

"Captain," the Lieutenant's voice rang out, "Major General Campbell will be ready to inspect your organization in" - he looked at his wrist-watch - "two hours."

"Very well, sir." Captain Anderson returned the Lieutenant's salute. He, again, rubbed his eyes and turned to Sergeant Walker.

"Walker, have the men got up immediately, police up, and be ready to stand inspection in one hour and a half."

"Yes, sir." Sergeant Walker saluted sharply

"And Walker."

"Sir!"

"Pass the word on to the Sergeants of the other platoons. We officers have had a pretty hard night of it and I am going to try and get some sleep before the General returns."

Sergeant Walker ran through the bunk houses informing the other platoon Sergeants of their fortune.

That finished, he returned to his own bunk house, and, starting along the row of sleeping men, unerringly picked the Corporals of the squads and instructed them to awaken their squads.

Soon the bunk house was filled with cries of: "Up you come, you dopes. Rise and shine."

"Is everybody up?"

"Then fall in beside your bunks and answer to roll-call."

"Now," said Sergeant Walker, as he finished roll-call, "you've got jist one hour to police up and be ready to stand general inspection. Snap into it."

Meeting between the platoon and general officers had been very limited; each man was overwhelmed with awe at the thought of a Major-General inspecting him. The scene changed to one of frenzied activity.

Dampened rags were rubbed over the stocks of the rifles; the rifle bores were cleaned, their chambers, trigger-guard, and other metal pieces were meticulously brushed; knives were put into use to scrape off the mud from the shoes and clothing; the blankets were stripped from the bunks and rolled into neat packs; water was found and stubbles of beard disappeared magically under the sharp edges of razors, or else were hidden by heavy coatings of talcum powder.

An hour afterward the platoon was in line in front of the bunk house. Clicking his heels sharply, for he wore barracks shoes because his tender feet were unable to stand the heavy hob-nails issued to the soldier, Sergeant Walker halted before his command.

"Ha-right, dress." His diaphragm, which had been expanded, noticeably contracted as he uttered the command of execution. "Back just a trifle, Green. Move your feet . . . Come out, you man in the third squad of the front rank. Nobody's going to hurt you. Step out a bit. Dammit, move your feet. All right, Corporal Phillips, suck in your gut and throw out your chest. There . . . The moment was tense. "Stea-a-dy. Front." The left arms of the men were dropped smartly at their sides.

Lieutenant Harris, traces of sleepiness still in his eyes, came forward and took charge of the platoon. He thrust out his arm, exposing a small gold wrist-watch beneath his cuff. Giving the watch an off-hand glance, he raised his voice: "All right, men if you'll keep one foot in place I'll give you at ease. No talking." He walked to the rear of the platoon and began to converse with Sergeant Walker.

"Pipe down, you men, or you'll stand at attention!" Sergeant Walker commanded.

The Company Commander came. He stood before the company and received the Lieutenant's report. The company, which had been called to attention during the formality, was given at ease again. They stood shuffling their feet. One man surreptitiously drew from his pocket a piece of tobacco, bit loose a small portion of it and returned it, unnoticed.

An hour passed.

Along the line voices were heard to remark: "Are we gonna stay here all day? They might at least feed us before they break us out like this. A hell of a note."

Sergeant Walker rose grandly to the occasion. "Shut up, you bunch of agitators. I'll drill you till your shoes fall off."

"You wouldn't have to drill me much. Mine already have holes in them," someone remarked.

"Who said that?" Sergeant Walker was furious.

Lieutenant Harris stepped in front of the platoon and called the men to attention.

The second hour had passed.

A huge touring-car rounded the road and stopped. The Company Commander, in magnificent tones, commanded them: "Company at-ten-shun. Open ranks. March . . . Steady . . . Front."

He saluted Major-General Campbell, who had stepped out of the touring-car.

"How do you do, Captain?"

The Major-General, followed by his Lieutenant, followed by another, followed by the Company Commander, followed by the Sergeant, walked pompously along the line of the front rank. The driver of the touring-car sent his car smoothly between the ranks. At the other end of the company the car stopped. The Major-General, the Lieutenant with the curled mustache, and another officer, climbed in and the car spurted away.

The ranks were closed, the company was reprimanded for its slovenly appearance and dismissed.

CHAPTER SIX

Instead of measuring up to the platoon's conception of a rest camp, the routine was more like that of an intensive training camp. Each morning there were close-order drills, at which Sergeant Walker would distinguish himself by giving the platoon a difficult command: "To the rear, squads right about, right by squads, on right into line," he would proudly call off, ending with a very sharp "March!" For a while the platoon obeyed, and in an orderly manner carried out the command. One day, after Sergeant Walker had given the command of execution, the right guide of the platoon continued to march forward.

"What's the matter there, right guide? Can't you hear? Platoon, halt!"

Sergeant Walker hurried forward and stood before the guide. "What the devil is the matter? You ought to know that command by this time."

The right guide spoke: "There is no such command anymore."

"What do you mean? How dare you!" Sergeant Walker was exasperated. The guide was calm.

"We're under army regulations and you can't give more than one command at a time."

"When I get you up before the Company Commander for insubordination you'll think otherwise. Wipe that smile off your face, you men back there."

Sergeant Walker maneuvered them about until he had exhausted all of the commands that he could think of. Then he ordered double-time, and they ran around the field, in the burning hot sun, for fifteen minutes. It would have been longer, but the Company Commander, passing by, ordered the platoon to be halted, and, calling the Sergeant aside, told him to stop.

Such occurrences served the platoon well, for the men were angered and taken away from their more intimate troubles. In the evening the rifts of the day would be forgotten as they would sit around the bunk house and listen to old Ollie Parker strum the guitar that the platoon had bought for him.

It was late in May, and the rains that had marked the springtime had almost stopped. It was evening, and a dull yellow moon soared gracefully above shoals of white, vaguely formed clouds. In the heavens the disk seemed like a ship, rocking a trifle as it rose over a sea of fluffy cotton.

Outside the bunk house members of the platoon stretched full length on the thick, soft grass, and listened to old Parker pick tentatively at the strings of his guitar.

"Play us somep'n sad an' boozy, Parker."

"Naw, play *The Little Marine Went Sailing Away*."

"Give us *If I Had the Wings of an Angel*."

"Can't play nothin' without a drink," Parker informed the group. "Now, if I was back in Muskogee tonight I'd go in M'Gittis' saloon and say 'Fill 'em up agin, M'Gittis, all night . . .' Ain't nobody got a drink?" he broke off plaintively.

"Well, I got a little wine you can have, Parker. It's in my canteen."

"Wine? You call that red hog-wash wine? I like hooch, anyway."

There was a pause.

"Go and git your damned old wine." In the evenings when there was no occupation for the platoon, Parker rated equally with President Wilson.

The wine was brought and Ollie Parker drank well. He wiped his mouth with the back of his hand, emitted a satisfied "Ah," and began:

> Oh, meet me, oh, meet me, tonight, love,
> Oh, meet me in the garden alone.
> For I've a sad story to tell you,
> A story that's never been told.

Parker solemnly chanted the last lines and stopped.

"I can't play no more. That damned wine makes me dry."

The conversation turned upon decent prostitutes and honest gamblers, a discussion over which Jay Edwards alone had taken the affirmative every time.

"You betcha there can be decent gold-diggers. And honest gamblers, too," he was saying. "What's so funny about that? They're nothing but ways of making a living."

"Yes, but, Edwards," one of the men interrupted, "if a woman goes around and sleeps with everybody she can't be very decent, can she?"

"As decent as your damned society whores, every time. Now look here. A woman gits married. And then she leaves her husband." He stopped.

"Got that? Well, she marries another guy and then another. Now, how is she any better than a regular gold-digger?"

"This ain't no place to talk about things like that. No place at all. You all bettah be prayin' to Gawd that this hyah wah'll soon be ovah," said Morrow.

Mercifully, the officer of the day walked by and ordered them off to bed.

On Decoration Day[10] all of the units of the regiment were marched to Regimental Headquarters and crowded upon the lawn in front of the building occupied by the Colonel and his staff. After waiting perhaps an hour, the Regimental Chaplain, pot-bellied, short-legged, and wholly bald, addressed the soldiers. Vaguely they comprehended that this was the day when fallen heroes were to be especially revered, and that it should also be a day of silent prayer and commemoration for the souls of those who were about to die. Half of the audience heard not a word, and fully three-quarters of them would not have been interested if they had.

The platoons filed out and marched over the dusty road for several miles back to their quarters. In some manner the commemoration address of the Regimental Chaplain left the members of the platoon gloomy. For a long while, as they marched along, there was no sound save for the muffled tramp of feet on the thickly dust-coated road.

Finally Phillips ended the silence: "You know, fellows, the Regimental Chaplain was right. All of us haven't so damned long to live."

"Come out of it, you gloom bug."

---

[10] 30 May to honor those who died in the American Civil War.

"Why do you care? You'll be alive to spit on all of our graves. You should worry."

"By God, Phillips is right. I was up at Battalion H.Q. night before last, and I heard some old boy tellin' Major Adams that we were goin' back to the front pretty damn quick."

"Pretty damn quick? I guess we are. The Battalion runner told me that we was shovin' off for the front tonight," Morrow contributed.

To all this conversation Bloomfield, a New York Jew, who had given his occupation as a travelling salesman, listened eagerly without appearing especially to do so. His prominent, fluid-brown eyes were turned upon Morrow, and they continued furtively to watch him while he spoke.

"You know, they say it's hell up at the front now. The Squareheads[11] have busted through and the Frogs are fallin' back as fast as they can. I betcha," Morrow continued excitedly, "that we'll be up to the front in less than - in less than a week."

"Yeh, an' they say they cut ya where you don' wanna be cut."

"Pipe down, you men back there. Who gave you permission to talk?" Sergeant Walker called.

"Who the hell gave you permission to give us permission to talk?" someone indistinctly asked.

The platoon plodded along, their thoughts too taken up with the matter at hand - arriving at their quarters, being fed, and going to sleep - to give further thought to the eventuality of being killed.

---

[11] Term used for a German soldier due to the square configuration of the helmet as compared to the round helmet of the Americans.

When they swung into their quarters, the fumes of the concoction which they had cheerfully and not inaccurately entitled slum were apparent to them. It assaulted their nostrils, but it was acceptable to empty stomachs.

They sat around; some were cross-legged on the ground, others sat upon dried manure piles, with their mess-gears half filled with slum by their sides.

Garrett and Morrow were seated together.

"What was that," Garrett asked, "you were saying about going to the front? Was that just general orders from the latrine, or was it straight?"

"Ah jist told you what I heard, Garrett. Some old guy told Major Adams that we'd be gittin' out of here damn quick. That's all I know. But say, it wouldn't surprise me none if we went any time. Even tonight."

"Oh, hell, no. Not tonight. I'm too damned tired to move. I'd go to the first-aid station, if we shoved off tonight." Garrett was despondent.

Morrow shrugged his shoulders and once more attacked his slum. A moment later the Company Commander walked toward the place where the men were eating. He was followed by the First Sergeant. He approached Sergeant Walker.

"Sergeant," he said, "have your platoon make up their packs and stand by. Let no one go to bed, and be ready to leave at any moment."

"Yes, sir," said Sergeant Walker.

"By God, Morrow, you were right, you uncanny bastard. It's tonight that we leave," said Garrett.

Midnight. Long rubber ponchos were drawn over recumbent figures; heads were pillowed by packs; sleep remained impervious to Allied propaganda. There was a tearing noise as a rifle exploded.

The Company Commander came running out of the farmhouse, where he and the other officers lodged with the farmer and his family. "What the devil are you men trying to do?"

"Somebody's shot himself, Captain."

The First Sergeant followed, bringing with him a flashlight. He hurried to the place where a group of men had gathered. Pushing through, he directed the rays of the flashlight toward the body. It was Bloomfield. He had placed the butt of the rifle on the ground, and with the muzzle pressed against his throat, had forced the trigger with his toe. There he lay, with one shoe off and the blood streaming from a hole in his jaw.

CHAPTER SEVEN

The platoon assembled and joined the rest of the company along the road. They marched off in the darkness, melting in with the immeasurable stream of olive drab that swelled at every cross-road.

Up and down the hills they marched, evenly wearing away the distance that lay between themselves and their destination. In the night there were no directions, no cool and mysterious little cafes to draw their attention from placing one foot after the other. Marching at night, Garrett thought, was much easier than marching in the daytime, provided that it was not too dark and the roads were not too slippery. Everything was serene. And it remained so until the man behind you stepped on your heel or until a small, carnivorous louse, a yellow one with a large black speck in the middle of its back, commenced to crawl under your arm or upon your chest. But after ten or fifteen miles, marching even at night was oppressive.

At the bottom of the millionth valley they passed through, lay the town. Along the road, leading up the hill on the other side, horizon-blue motor-trucks stood and waited.

The platoon came to a halt in one of the streets, the butts of their rifles clattering on the cobblestones. It had been quite dark a moment ago, but dawn had come hurriedly, and now Garrett could see the great number of troops that were preparing to embark.

He turned to Rogers, a confessed virgin and the only person in the platoon who boasted of it. "It will be hours before our turn comes. Let's sneak off somewhere and lie down."

"Oh, no," Rogers decisively answered. "You can't tell how soon we'll be called. And then we may get into trouble."

"You'll probably get into trouble if you go up to the front, too. You'd better go up to the Company Commander and tell him you're sick."

Rogers failed to reply, and Garrett, glancing around, noticed the officers were not in sight.

"Oh, Morrow . . . Morrow. Let's go find a haymow."

"Oh-o, Garrett's gittin' to be a wildcat. He wants to leave his little platoon. All right, come on, Garrett." Every time Morrow talked his voice reminded Garrett of a crippled professional beggar.

They slipped off their packs, dropped them at their feet, and dodged around a street corner.

No sooner had they passed out of sight of the platoon than Garrett exclaimed: "Well, I'm damned. Ol' Bennett. Have you got a drink?"

"Hello, Garrett." Bennett put out a hand that was like a dead fish. "I've got a little rum."

"Well, who wants anything better than rum? Morrow, meet an old friend of mine, Oscar Bennett. Bennett, this is Clayton Morrow, the best gambler in the regiment."

"How do you do?" Bennett again produced the clammy insensible hand.

"What kind of a job have you got that you can be traipsing around the streets like this with a bottle of rum on your hip?" demanded Garrett.

"Oh, I'm the Colonel's interpreter. I order the ham, eggs, drinks, and women for him."

"That's not a bad job," Garrett admitted. "Now, how about the hooch?"

A full quart bottle was brought into view. Bennett uncorked it and passed it. It went from Garrett to Morrow, to Bennett, to Garrett, again to Morrow, to Bennett and around once more. Then it was thrown into the gutter, empty.

"I tell you, Garrett, and you, too, Mr. Morrow, that we are going to see strange things before very long. What would you say if I told you that the Germans had broken through the French lines and were headed for Paris?"

"I'd say," said Morrow, "that I don't wondah a damn bit. Them damn Frogs is always asleep. They're too pretty to kill a mosquito."

Bennett, taking hold of Garrett's shoulder-strap and holding it grimly, set his mouth with firmness, and, with a full pause between each word, said: "Garrett I mean it. There's going to be hell to pay in a few days."

"Well, why are you worrying?" Garrett answered. "You won't be in any of it."

"Come on, Garrett, we'd better go." People were beginning to open the shutters of the houses on either side of the street, and both men began to wonder how long they had been away from the platoon.

They hurried back, arriving just as the platoon had started slowly to move forward.

No one seemed to have the least notion of the direction in which the camions were moving. Though some of the men who had been reading a recent copy of the Paris edition of the Chicago *Tribune,* believed them to be headed for the Somme, where, it was said, there was heavy fighting; others believed that they were on their way to relieve the First American Division, which a few days earlier had attacked at Cantigny. Apparently the trip was to last an extraordinarily long time, for each squad had been apportioned two days' extra rations before entraining. The drivers of the camions were Anamites[12], and, as purveyors of information, were
as useful in that respect as so many professional silent men of the President's cabinet.

With twenty men in each camion the caravan bumped and thundered along the road all day. At night they stopped only a few minutes to allow the soldiers to prepare themselves for a still longer journey.

Late the next afternoon they passed a city which they decided was Meaux. The men in the camions did not know where they were going, but they did know that it was in the direction of the front. In the town the streets were crowded with wagons, carts, domestic animals, and people. Comforters were thrown out over the hard pavement, and families were lying on them, resting. It seemed as if the entire city was so filled with people that one other person could not get in.

The camions hurried through, while the men inside, leaning forward, shouted couchay[13] and other words of which they did not know the meaning whenever they saw any youngish women.

---

[12] French from the Annamese Mountains.
[13] A vulgar way of relating to intimacy.

Leaving Meaux, the spirit of attack already seemed to be entering the men. Outside the city they met an old man with a patriarchal beard, seated upon his household goods, which were piled upon a little cart driven by a mule. Beside the cart walked a woman that might have been either his wife or his daughter. The old man looked as if he were crying. His mouth was drawn back into a querulous pucker and his hands rested limply in his lap.

"Don't you worry, pappy. We'll get your home back for you," called a voice from one of the camions. The sentiment was taken up and voiced by a great number. Through the warm glow of the spirit of the crusader that it gave them, all other emotions were submerged.

Mirrors in ornate frames apparently had a special significance for the refugees. Not one of them but had carefully salvaged his mirror and was displaying it, safely bound to the bed-clothing with which the cart was loaded down. Every one of the refugees seemed also to have a large feather bed, and among the property that they were carrying away from their deserted homes was often to be noticed a round glass cover under which was a wedding-cake or a carved miniature of an old-fashioned man and maid dancing a minuet.

It was night, and many of the men had gone to sleep. The camions stopped abruptly, and the awakened men, trying vainly to unlimber their stiffened muscles, laboriously made their way to the ground.

Garrett had been one of the first men to leave the camion. Now he walked around in front of it. Funny, there were no other camions before him! He ran to the rear and down the road a few paces. No camions there either.

"Hey, fellows! we're lost."

"Lost? And up here? What the hell are we going to do?"

"I don't give a damn if we are lost. I need a vacation, anyway."

"Pipe down, damn it. You can't tell how near we are to the German lines."

"Yeh, and that Frog a drivin' might be a German spy. We better watch out."

They were still talking when Sergeant Powell arrived. He had left the truck when it stopped. Walking ahead, he had found a deserted village.

"Well, fellahs. You better get down out of there and come with me. There are plenty of places to sleep right up ahead, and as it looks like we're lost, that's what we'd better do."'

Sergeant Powell always talked as if he were about to chuckle. Ever since the platoon had been formed Sergeant Powell had been held up to the entire company, and often to the battalion, as the best-looking soldier readily to be found. Even in the trenches his nails were manicured, the nails of his long, sensitive fingers. His small pointed mustache looked as if it had been freshly waxed. His puttees were rolled neatly about his smart-looking legs. And he could drink all night, and, to the eye, not be affected by it.

"We'll foller Powell any place, won't we, guys?"

"You're damned right."

They gathered together their equipment and started after him down the road. It was a very small town and had been evacuated two days before. No matter if the feather beds had been taken away, there was plenty of dry hay to sleep on.

Morning came and Sergeant Powell was awake and engaged in rousing the men. After they had all been found, he assembled them on the street and issued orders: "Now you men can do what you please. Only don't break anything. We are going to stay here until somebody comes for us. There ought to be plenty of food around, and you ought to know what to do."

There was plenty of food. Plump-legged pullets stalked temptingly before them, and young Dempsy, who heretofore had never distinguished himself in any way, developed an uncanny aptitude of snaring them with a swoop of his left arm, clutching them neatly by the leg. Nearly all of the cellars contained potatoes, and wine was not uncommon.

Into a chateau which presumably belonged to the overlord of the village the party carried their food. The pullets had been prepared for frying, potatoes were sizzling in a large kettle of grease, a table had been laid with a crisp linen cloth.

The party was seated around a large table. Upon the linen cloth were china plates and bright knives and forks. In the center were dishes piled high with fried chicken and potatoes. A salad brightened the menu. Wine-glasses and tumblers were filled and dust-covered bottles stood near at hand, ready to replenish them.

"This is what you might call the life of Riley." Sergeant Powell spoke with his soft voice that almost broke into a chuckle.

"I'll tell the world. Jist like New York."

"Gittin' lost ain't hard to take. Jist think of the rest of the outfit, snappin' into it whenever Walker opens his yap."

The glasses were emptied and refilled. It was a religious ceremony.

"Now, if some of them dames we seen at Meaux was up here."

Suddenly Garrett started to laugh, long and loudly.

"What you laughin' at? Is there anything funny in my wantin' a little company? 'Course these Frog gals ain't as nice as . . ."

"No, no. It wasn't that at all. But we were going to save these people's homes - and now we're killing their chickens."

"You can't be so damned finicky. This is war."

"He's right, Garrett." Perry nodded sagely. "If we didn't get it the Squareheads would."

The party, all but Powell, tilted back in their chairs, their tunics unbuttoned and their belts unfastened. Their eyes having proved larger than their appetites, much of the food remained on the table untouched. But there was room in their bellies for wine, and bottle after bottle was opened and emptied.

"There," said Perry, pointing to an empty bottle, "is a good soldier. He has done his duty and he is willing to do it again."

Foolishly, the men raised their hands to their forehead in a gesture of homage.

CHAPTER EIGHT

They lurched out into the street. The day was hot and still, and the men, exhilarated by the wine and satiated with the food, were planning for other banquets as sumptuous. Around the corner of the crooked street marched an orderly, wearing his inevitable look of having the responsibility of the war on his shoulders.

"Are you men from C Company of the Sixth?"

"You're damned right we are, buddy. Have you got anything to say about it?"

"No. Only you'd better hurry up and join them or you'll be up for a shot for desertion."

"Why, whaddya mean? Where are they?" Several men spoke at once.

"Well," said the orderly importantly, "they were getting ready to go over the top when I left."

"Great, Christ!" Powell lamented. "We'd better hurry. Lead the way, orderly."

Flanked by rows of waving wheat, the party plodded along the dusty, narrow road.

"Now we are in it for sure," Garrett thought. "And me especially. If Major Adams hears about this I'll be hung higher than a kite." But he forgot the possibility of a court martial in his thinking of the platoon and of where they were and of where he was soon to be.

They found their outfit in a clump of woods, a little to the left of the road. In front of them was the spectacle of what a French village looked like after it had been subjected to long-range artillery fire for three days. The spire of the little church had been blown off; there was not a house or barn whose side or roof had not been pierced by a shell. Mortar and glass were strewn about the streets, where they mingled with articles of household use. Beside the door of one of the houses a Red Cross flag had been fastened, and inside the medical detachment were making preparations for visitors.

Ol' Parker sat hunched up, his helmet over his eyes, looking down at his heavy shoes. Phillips, a lightweight boxer from Pennsylvania, was attacking a tin of corned beef, trying to open it with his bayonet. Garland, from Cleveland, who carried a khaki-colored handkerchief which he had used for three months, sat with his arms around his knees, his eyes looking far away and moist.

"What's the matter, Parker?" Garrett called, anxious somehow to make himself again a part of the platoon as soon as he could.

"Oh, this damned war makes me sick. Always movin' around. They never let you stay one place a minute."

"Join the army and see the world," someone called.

"Through the door of a boxcar," someone else amended.

"You'll be up here long enough, old fellow. You ought to come from my part of the country, Parker. They do a lot of cutting and shooting there."

"Yeh." Parker was ironic. "They do a lot of cuttin' and shootin'. They cut around the corner and shoot for home."

Phillips laughed exultantly. He felt that at last the time he had given to training was to be of some purpose. He abandoned trying to open the tin of meat because he feared that he would dull his bayonet. And he wanted it to be sharp, so sharp. Those dirty Huns. He drew his finger along the edge of the shiny piece of steel. That would cut, all right. That wouldn't be deflected by a coat-button from piercing the intestines.

Lieutenant Harris, bent forward as usual, the end of his nose wiggling nervously, came among them with Sergeants Powell and Walker.

"There won't be any smoking or any matches lit after dark tonight, fellows. We are only about a mile from the German front line. As near as I can make out they are advancing and it is our job to stop them. We'll probably move forward some time after dark, so have your stuff by your side."

"When do we eat? Won't we get any chow all night?"

"The galley is in the town back of us. They are cooking up some slum, and it ought to be brought up here pretty soon." Harris walked away.

"There's nothing like a good kick in the face to make you forget your little troubles." Perry summed up the feeling of the platoon.

Phillips, industriously, was working the bolt of his rifle back and forth, pouring drops of oil in the chamber and upon the lock. He leaned toward Garrett and remarked in an undertone: "Garrett, old fellow, if Kyle Phillips doesn't earn a Croix de Guerre tomorrow his mother will be without a son."

"What do you want one of those things for, Phillips? You can buy 'em for five francs."

"But you can't earn one of them with five francs."

"But what do you want with one of them? What good are they?"

Garrett, perhaps, was insincere. One might want a decoration and be delighted to have it, but intentionally to go after it appalled him in the light of absurdity.

As Lieutenant Harris departed, each man drew inside himself. Merely to observe them, one would have believed that they were concerned with profound thoughts. A Y.M.C.A. secretary would have told himself that the men were thinking of their homes and families, praying to God, and the Y.M.C.A. General Pershing would have charged them with possessing a fierce, burning desire to exterminate the Germans. The Regimental Chaplain - he had come to the Regiment from a Methodist pulpit - would have said that they were repenting of their sins and supplicating God for mercy.

While it was yet light Sergeants Walker and Powell and Lieutenant Harris discussed aloud the plans that had been tentatively given them for the night, but as objects in their line of vision lost their distinctness and became vague, mysterious figures, they lowered their voices to a whisper. Lieutenant Harris peered at his wrist-watch.

"It's time to go. Better break out the men, Walker." Sergeant Walker crept along the road to the clump of woods where the platoon was huddled.

"All right, men," he whispered hoarsely; "it's time to shove off. Has everybody got his trench tools?"

"I've lost my shovel."

"I didn't mean you, Dempsey. You'd lose your head if it wasn't fastened on. Is anyone missing any of their equipment?"

There was no answer.

"All right. Form in a column of twos and follow me." Sergeant Walker started off, and the men, who had risen, fell in behind him.

Until this time all had been quiet, but now the machine-guns, unmistakably Maxims,[14] began an intermittent fire. It seemed to be a signal for the rifles, for now and again one of them would crack pungently somewhere in the dark.

The platoon was marching cautiously over the hill to the town in front of them.

"Stand fast!" Sergeant Powell called out sharply. A rocket was fired, rose high in the air, and then, the parachute spreading out, floated slowly to earth, lighting up the ground for several hundreds of yards on each side. As soon as it had reached the ground the platoon marched on. They passed through the town, and, as they were leaving, a covey of shells whirred softly over their heads and landed among the ruins with a terrific explosion. The walls that remained seemed to reverberate. It sounded as if they were rocking back and forth from the concussion.

At the military crest of the hill the platoon stopped, joined on its left by the rest of the Company. The Company Commander walked along the line, repeating, so that each man could hear: "You'll have to hurry and dig in, men. It's three hours until dawn, and if you haven't got yourselves a place of safety by that time you will be unfortunate."

---

[14] German machine-guns.

The men threw off their packs, unstrapped their trench tools, and set to work to make holes in the ground sufficiently deep to protect their bodies from rifle fire and from pieces of flying shell. As there were only four men in each squad equipped with trench tools, the other half commenced digging with their bayonets and scraping the dirt from the hole that they were making with the lid of their mess gear. But they worked furiously, and with the aid of the Company Commander and all of the sub-officers, which consisted in telling them that they had just so much longer until dawn, each pair of men had made for themselves a hole in the ground from which they could manipulate their rifles without exposing their bodies to direct fire.

When dawn broke the company presented to the enemy a slightly curved front of newly made holes, with the dirt thrown up in front of them for further protection.

Across the valley, perhaps five-hundred yards, was a thickly wooded hill, from which, as the light strengthened, the platoon could see figures running out into the field and then back again among the trees. Then, to the right, the Hotchkiss machine-guns[15] began their wavering patter.

From another wood, in front and to the left of the platoon, ran soldiers in frayed and dirty horizon-blue uniforms. Walker pointed to the wooded hill where the scurrying figures had been seen. "Boche?" he asked.

"Oui, Boche," the men in the soiled uniforms answered.

"Boche, Paris?" someone asked.

"Oui." The Frenchman shrugged his shoulders. "Ce ne fait rien."[16]

---

[15] French machine-guns.
[16] Loose translation: It does not matter.

Doubtless the Frenchmen, Garrett thought, did not care; for seven days they had been forced to fall back, slowly and with heavy losses. There was little opportunity for sleep; and food, despite the conscientious efforts of the French cooks, was difficult to procure. They felt beaten.

Another group of French soldiers hurried out of the woods, and, as the others had done, disappeared through the ruins of the village.

It was quite light now, and the German artillery awoke. The first salvo of shells struck in the town. The second fell in the field to the right of the village.

Overhead the motor of an airplane whirred. Under its wings were painted large black crosses. It fired a signal, rose again in the air, wheeled, and flew back.

"Duck your heads," shouted Sergeant Powell, pulling a cigarette from his pocket. "They've got our range for sure."

They had. A moment later a number of shells began a leisurely journey in the direction of the platoon. As they approached they lost their tardiness and fell shrieking, like maddened demons, along the line of freshly dug dirt.

"Anybody get hit?" Sergeant Powell rose and looked around.

"Stretcher bearer on the right!" Garrett yelled.

CHAPTER NINE

In the hole next to Garrett's a curious thing had happened. A shell had grazed the top of the hole, buried itself in the dirt, and then back-fired. When the stretcher-bearers arrived they found that Green, one of the men in the hole, had part of his back torn off. Quickly they laid him prone on the stretcher and started for the town as swiftly as the weight of their burden would permit. The other man, Dempsey, was still crouched in the position he had assumed when Sergeant Powell called the warning.

Garrett jumped over beside him. "Dempsey," he called. Dempsey failed to respond. Garrett put his arm around him and lifted him up. Dempsey began to laugh horribly. Then great tears coursed through the mud on his cheeks.

"Dempsey, what's the matter?"

Dempsey laughed again in the same manner. He had completely lost control of his muscles and would have fallen face downward, if Garrett had not held him up.

"Tell Lieutenant Harris that there's something the matter with Dempsey," Garrett shouted.

The word was passed along.

"Lieutenant Harris says for you to get somebody else and take him back to the first-aid station. He's probably shell-shocked."

"Oh, Thompson," Garrett called. "Come and help me take Dempsey back to the first-aid station."

"Aw, Garrett, I can't. I'm sick at my stomach. I couldn't help carry anything."

"Well, Morrow - come on, Morrow, you help me."

And Morrow got out of his hole, a few yards away, and ran over. Both men, one holding Dempsey's legs and the other his shoulders, waded into the stream of machine-gun bullets as they hurried the shell-shocked man to the dressing station.

In the village there was greater safety - cellars to hide in, and there to escape the flying pieces of shells that fell into the town at short intervals.

Garrett and Morrow rested for a moment, filled their canteens with water, and started back. Half-way to the platoon they found a Frenchman lying upon his back.

"A moi, a moi," he was groaning scarcely above a whisper.

"What's the mattah, buddy," Morrow asked.

". . . par le gaz . . . par le gaz."

"He says he's been gassed, Morrow. Let's take him back, too."

"Here, buddy, do you want a drink of watah?" Morrow asked.

The Frenchman drank greedily.

"By God," Morrow said, "that's the first Frog I've ever seen that would drink water."

They carried the Frenchman to the dressing station, and after they had explained to the Captain of the Medical Corps where they had found him, in what a desperate condition he was, and that there was nothing else to do with him, the Frenchman was finally accepted.

"We can't fill this place up with all kinds of people," the Medical Officer objected. "We'll have a hard-enough time taking care of our own men in a few minutes."

Morrow, disgusted, emitted a stream of tobacco juice, shrugged his shoulder, turned on his heel.

"Come on, Garrett, let's get back where there's real soldiers."

Their hearts racing madly, they reached their holes without being struck by the machine-gun bullets that sang deadly songs all around. After the first terrific salvo, the German artillery, for some unknown reason, had stopped.

The skirmishing on the right, which the platoon had witnessed in the early morning, seemed to have been carried within the woods. A few waves of pigmy-like figures had walked slowly toward the wooded hill, and by the time their lines arrived, although considerably thinned, the gray defenders of the hill were to be seen no more.

Now that they were no longer targets, Garrett walked over to where Powell was squatted in his hole.

"This is a hell of a note, isn't it, Powell? To have to lie like this all day and not get to fire a shot?"

"You'll get a chance to fire plenty of shots, damn it. Some poor fool is making our regiment attack without a barrage. Did you see the outfit over on the right that went up that hill? That was the Third Battalion, and I'll bet there's not a company left outa the whole bunch. Well, we'll go over most any time."

"But, Powell, that's murder, not to have a barrage. What can these fool officers be thinking of?"

"Glory," Powell answered.

Late in the afternoon the Company Commander passed the word along the line that the men would be permitted to eat one of their boxes of hard bread, but nothing else.

"Who the hell wants to eat any of that damned stuff?"

"God, my hardtack laid in the trenches for six weeks, and even them damned rats wouldn't eat it."

The platoon had recovered its spirits, its morale, as the white-collared fighters for democracy often spoke of it.

As night was coming on, a noise was heard in the grass between the men and the ruined village. It coughed tentatively, then decisively.

"Who's back there?"

"A runner from Battalion Headquarters," the voice answered cautiously. "Don't shoot."

"Oh, come ahead."

"What the hell are you afraid of?"

"We're not as fierce as we look."

"Where's your Company Commander?" the voice asked.

"He went over to ask the Squareheads to stop shootin'. There's a man here that's got a headache," Morrow informed the voice.

"No, where is he, fellows?" By this time the voice had become Bennett. Garrett recognized him.

"Hello, Bennett."

"Oh!" Bennett walked over to Garrett's hole and jumped in. "Hello, Garrett."

"What are you doing here? I thought you were interpreter for the Colonel."

"I was, Garrett, but I drank too much one night and he fired me," Bennett answered sadly.

"What do you want with the Company Commander?"

"I don't know whether I should tell you."

"Hell, I'll find it out in a minute, anyway."

"Well, your Company is to move to another position as soon as it gets dark enough."

"What for? Are we going to attack?"

"I don't know, Garrett, I'm sure. Where's your Captain?"

"He's over between the Third and Second platoons, about fifteen holes down that way."

Bennett got up, and, stooping over until his head was parallel with his hips, trotted in the direction Garrett had indicated.

An hour later the orders came for the men to sling their packs and be ready to move again. And great was the outcry when the men heard the news.

"Are we going to dig up the whole of France?"

"I'll get my old man to buy some ploughs, if we are. I wasn't cut out to be a ditch digger."

"This is a hell of a note. Diggin' a hole for one day. I was jist gittin' mine so's I could sleep in it."

The Company lined up in single file and marched off.

After maneuvering around for a couple of hours they came to another woods. On the way they had been joined by a section of the machine-gun company that was attached to their Battalion. In a measure, this annexation was responsible for their slow progress. There were the carts to be hidden, and then the men of the machine-gun detail carried their guns and their ammunition in their arms. But they were halted at last, and amid much muttering and cursing were shooed into the woods and told that they might go to sleep for the night.

It was noon of the next day before they received any food. Then a detail had to be sent back to the village after it. And when they returned they brought with them cold boiled potatoes, cold coffee, and black French bread.

"Don't eat too many of these damned potatoes," Morrow warned all and sundry. "I was ridin' on a boxcar for three days once, and I didn't have nothin' else to eat, an' I got col' sores all over my mouth from eaten too many potatoes."

Cigarettes were scarce, so the butts of them were passed around and in that way shared by all.

The firing during the day was slight. Scattered rifle fire was heard on both sides, but the artillery was dumb. The men spent the day speculating upon whether their own artillery would arrive and get into position before they were ordered to attack.

Time after time Phillips nervously paced the length of the woods. He had done all that he could to his rifle. The bolt worked smoothly with a satisfying click. The bore had been swabbed free of the oil, which had been put there to keep the metal from rusting. The chamber held five meticulously clean shells and there was one in the bore.

Sergeants Lark and Walker were telling each other of what they used to do on the outside, by which phrase they meant before they had enlisted. Sergeant Powell was cursing because there was no water to be had. His canteen was half empty, and he knew better than not to hoard water. He decided that he would have to shave without water, and this angered him still more. Then he divided the water equally, using a portion for lather.

Thus, they passed the day.

CHAPTER TEN

To the weary platoon, their thinned ranks huddled all day long in the small clump of woods, night came on slowly and inexorably. The sun had disappeared, and, one by one, elf-like stars became apparent, twinkling like shaking jewels through the black curtain of the heavens. At sunset orders had been received for the platoon to be prepared to leave at any moment. Their rifles were lying by their sides, the men were sprawled on the damp ground, their heads resting on their combat packs.

Someone touched a lit match to a cigarette. It glowed softly in the darkness, a bright, inquisitive eye.

"Put out that God-damned light," Lieutenant Harris whispered hoarsely. "Do you want us all to get shot up?"

Soon at the edge of the woods the branches were parted and a tense voice called: "Where is Lieutenant Harris?"

It was a messenger from Battalion Headquarters carrying orders for the platoon to move. The summons was passed along from squad to squad, a disagreeable secret hurriedly disposed of. The men slung their packs and, holding their rifles in front of them, filed slowly and carefully out of the woods to form in a column of twos.

Lieutenant Harris in front and Sergeant Powell in rear - as if, Garrett thought, some of the men were thinking of deserting - the men marched off, joining the other platoons in the middle of the field.

Lieutenant Harris called: "Pass the word along to keep quiet; we're within hearing distance of the front lines."

On both sides the artillery was silent. Occasionally a machine-gun would fire a string of bullets the sound of which died in the stillness without an echo.

The men dragged slowly on, their legs soaked around the knees from the dew nestling on the tall wheat. For perhaps a mile they had marched, and the platoon, like a sensitive instrument, was beginning to have an unaccountable perception of danger, when shoes were heard swishing through the heavy wheat, and a voice said: "Turn around, you damned fools. Do you want to walk straight into the German trenches!"

The men breathed relievedly. Apparently they were not going immediately to attack. Recovering, they began audibly to curse the Lieutenant.

"The dirty German spy. What the hell does he think he's doin'?"

"Ought to be back at Battalion H.Q. with the rest of the dummies."

Lieutenant Harris remained grimly silent.

They were coming to another woods, solid black in the shifting black of night, and within a few yards of its fringes some officers stepped out and halted them.

"All right, here you are."

"Lieutenant, swing your men right in here and don't let anyone get out of the woods."

The men backed in among the trees and lay down, their packs, raising their shoulders from the ground, protecting them from the moisture. They lay silent, with their rifles cradled in their arms. No one seemed to mind the wet of the grass or the chill of the air. They were all silent and rather full of fear. Time was unknown. They might have been there a year - a minute - an eon.

Just as the trees, in a clump of woods perhaps a mile away, were beginning to come out against the sluggish sky like sharp, delicate etchings, the batteries awoke. After the first flock-of-shells, sounding like black, screaming spirits, were fired, the men in the woods were fully aroused and many of them were standing.

"Uh-h-h, did you hear that bunch of sandbags?"

"They sounded as if they came from a thousand miles."

Another salvo was fired, the shells droning lazily over the heads of the men and crashing terrifically more than a mile distant.

And then the smaller guns were unlimbered. The spiteful crack of the seventy-fives turned the funereal music into a scherzo. In retaliation the German batteries, the heavier ones, began, their shells flying high overhead.

Lieutenant Harris jumped up. "All right, Third Platoon. Up you come. Keep straight ahead and remember your three-yard interval. If anyone gets hit, let him lie." And then, as if he were uncertain, as if he wanted to convince himself of the actuality of the words he had just spoken, he added: "Those are the orders."

"I always knew they hated the Third," said Rogers, "but blamed if I knew they hated our guts so much that they put us in the first wave."

Garrett grinned stiffly. He was conscious of a feeling as if his face had become frozen and as if his chin were about to drop off. It hung slackly and his teeth came unnaturally together when he clinched his jaws. He tightened the chin-strap of his helmet, guarding against the chance of losing his chin. Next, his feet felt so awfully heavy. They would barely permit themselves to be lifted from the ground. They had become separate identities, and as he became conscious of them he felt them to be unfamiliar.

"Damn this mud," he told himself, though knowing well that there was no mud weighing down his feet.

After pounding away for fifteen minutes, the smaller artillery stopped. The whistle blew and the men advanced, stepping out in the open where the risen sun made them hideously conspicuous. The field separating the woods stretched far on either side, and was covered with green-stemmed wheat that reached hip-high.

Garrett, glancing over his shoulder, saw the rays of the sun flashing from the clean bayonets, the bayonets the men so often had jabbed into sacks of sand and straw.

The Sergeant in charge of the first wave set the pace, which was frightfully slow. Somewhere, farther down the line, men began to object to the snail-like progress.

"Yes," thought Garrett, "it's amusing that we walk so slowly when we are right out in plain sight." It struck him as odd that the line was not being fired upon, and then he explained it to himself by the notion that the heavy barrage had driven the enemy back. But what if it hadn't - what if the Germans are just waiting until we get right almost into the woods. Wouldn't that be a mess! And what a bore, this moping through the wet smoky wheat. He wondered whether his knees were bleeding. Curse it! His neck was stiff. Maybe he could limber it up if he shook his head . . . No, it couldn't be done. It didn't work.

The first wave entered the woods where the enemy was without firing a shot or being fired at. The second wave entered, and the third, and the fourth.

Phillips, parting the leaves with his sharp bayonet, unexpectedly looked out upon a clearing, and the sight he saw made him exclaim to the man next to him: "Oh, Christ, this must be some joke. Look at all those fellows asleep there."

In the clearing, lying flat on their backs, were five soldiers, their legs stretched out. They wore no shoes over their heavy woolen hose.

Garrett drew over toward him and looked.

"You better get down, you lumphead," Garrett cautioned; "they aren't asleep."

Together they crawled out toward the motionless figures. By this time Rogers, Parker, and Edwards had come to the clearing and started to follow.

"Je-sus, Phillips! Here's a fellow out of the Eighty-Third Company that I enlisted with. And he's dead as hell."

Rat-t-t-t . . .

It was a Maxim and the men dropped to their bellies.

"Hey, you poor fool, can't you shut up?" Thompson said. "That's a Maxim."

Garrett made for behind a tree as fast as he could crawl.

"Hey, Phillips," he called in an undertone, "where's the rest of the outfit?"

"I don't know," Phillips answered him. "That's the reason we come over here where you fellers are."

Garrett turned to Phillips. "By God, Phillips, we're lost!"

The machine-gun bullets shaved the bark from the trunk of the tree behind which Garrett was lying. He flattened out, his face pressed into the grass.

"Oh, Phillips, we're lost!"

But Phillips did not hear him. Possibly, he remembered what he had said earlier in the day. Possibly, he was really a hero. Possibly, he again saw himself as a little boy playing in the back yard. Whatever were his thoughts, he rose to one knee, and, after peering intently in the direction from which the bullets had come, he raised his rifle to his shoulder and sighted along the shining barrel.

Rat-t-t-t-tat.

A Maxim, but from an oblique direction, was firing, and Phillips sprawled on his face, his right arm falling over the shiny barrel of his rifle. Then other machine-guns rained their bullets into the clearing, and the men clawed at the ground in an effort to lower their bodies beneath the sweep of the lead.

"What'll we do, Garrett?" asked Edwards.

The tender green leaves from the trunk of the tree behind which Garrett was secure fluttered to the ground, clipped by the machine-gun fire.

"I don't know, but we can't stay here. Why don't you find the rest of the gang?"

"Why don't you?"

"Well . . ." Garrett started to crawl back from the clearing into the woods. After he had wriggled his body about fifty yards he rose to his feet and ran in the general direction of which he had last seen the Company. Breaking through the woods, he met Captain Anderson.

"Captain Anderson, there's a squad of us up there, and we're lost. We don't know what to do. The men are in a clearing, and they're afraid to move because they're right in sight of a nest of machine-guns. Do you know where the platoon is? What shall we do?"

And in a Shakespearian voice Captain Anderson told Garrett to return to his squad and lead them in a charge on the machine-gun nest.

"Yes, sir." Garrett turned and squirmed back through the woods to the clearing. "Like hell we'll advance," he thought, shivering; and cursed. "The God-damned idiot."

Garrett reached the clearing at the same time the German machine-guns momentarily stopped.

"Ja find 'em, Garrett?"

"No, but I saw Anderson. If we made a half circle back to the left we might find 'em."

"Sounds good enough to try."

CHAPTER ELEVEN

They were crawling, crawling on their bellies, in single file, when Morrow stopped and called with an exultant lilt in his voice:

"Oh-o, here's one Squarehead that's kissed his papa good-by. Right through the eye."

The men in rear veered off so as not to see the body, that even in death might still be dangerous. A short distance away someone was moaning weakly. Garrett stopped. "Another one of our guys hit, I betcha."

They crawled eagerly and yet fearfully toward the noises. Seen through the trees bandy-legged Private Franks was supporting the head of little Sanders and trying to get him to open his eyes. Beside him was Lieutenant Harris, saying: "You're crazy, Franks. The kid's gone, but we'll see if anything can be done."

Franks was softly calling: "Sanders, oh, Sanders, ain't you got anything to say?"

Garrett got to his feet and came beside the group that was staring at the dead face of Sanders.

"What's that? Little Sanders get it? Je's, that's bad."

And Morrow: "Poor little fellah. I give him a hunnerd francs the other day. But he sure is welcome to it."

Franks straightened his body, letting the head of Sanders touch the ground. Clinching his fist, he raised it above his head and shook it toward the woods: "We'll get you, you dirty -" He could not find the word with which he wanted to characterize the inhumanity of the Germans.

Harris grasped at his arm: "Get down, you damned fool. Do you want to get hit, too?"

The advance through the woods had begun in an orderly manner, but after reaching the more dense part the German machine-guns commenced firing and four men fell. The rest tramped on, unable to see the enemy. Suddenly they realized that they had broken contact between themselves and the platoon on their left. Going forward, they wedged themselves into the German lines and made a target for enfilade[17] fire. Then, little more to be done except get killed, they halted.

An orderly from Battalion Headquarters crawling through the woods carried with him the information for Captain Anderson that the company was to entrench for the night. When the news reached them the platoon failed even to comment. For once their garrulous selves were stilled. The realization that they were to spend a night freighted with experiences totally new, that through the darkness they were to be powerless to defend themselves, stunned them.

A curving line was described by Lieutenant Harris, and the men were deployed along it at intervals. They unslung their packs, their extra bandoliers of ammunition, and furiously began to dig holes in the ground deep enough for them to be in without exposing their bodies. Some used their hand shovels and picks, while others, more careless

---

[17] A volley of gunfire directed along a line from end to end.

with their equipment, used their bayonets to loosen the dirt and their mess-kit lids to scoop it out.

Dusk, like powder of old blue, sifted through the trees and wrapped the shallow burrows in a friendly mystery. In their fresh-made beds, peeping through the boughs with which they had covered the tops of their holes, the men waited.

Through the long night that stretched interminably before them they peered into the darkness, fancying, as they had in the trenches, that each tree trunk was an enemy. The least noise was sufficient for overworked nerves to press the trigger of a rifle and send a volley of bullets through the leaves of the trees. When they spoke it was in the smallest of whispers, and even so conversation was peculiarly lacking.

Garrett, at times, would think of a letter that his mother had written him in which she had offered to send him a quantity of cyanide of potassium. "You know, son," she had written, "this war is not like the war that grandpapa used to tell you about. Those frightful Germans have liquid fire and deadly gases, and it is only when I think of how you would suffer if you were burned by their infernal liquid fire that I offer to send it. If you want it, just mark a cross at the bottom of your next letter."

Garrett had not marked any cross. He had laughed at the notion at first, and then, as the months slipped by, he had forgotten entirely about it. Now he wondered if he had done wisely. Suppose he were shot like the fellow in the trench the other day? Or gassed as badly as the Frenchman whom he and Morrow had carried back to the first-aid station. Yes, it would have been comforting . . . but he revolted at the thought of poisoning himself. His early religion had been that a suicide does not better his condition. He simply would be answerable to his own demise. It would be hellish to live in the great beyond knowing he took the coward's way out, Garrett thought. Dear old Mother, how she had cried when he told her that he had enlisted and was to be sent almost immediately to France. "But, Mother, you were such a good patriot before I enlisted, and now you don't want me to go. What kind of patriotism is that?" he remembered having asked her. And how badly she had felt that he only spent an hour with her before he left for the training camp.

He was amused at the notion of digging holes to lie in. It is insulting, he thought, to ask a person to dig his own grave. It is barbaric.

The leaves of the trees were silvered above by the rays of the sun playing upon the dew. Morning had come.

Somewhere - and it seemed as if it were only ten yards away, a whistle blew a short and unfamiliar call.

"All right, Third Platoon!" Lieutenant Harris's voice was hoarse with excitement. "Forward, Third Platoon."

Hesitatingly and half-whimpering, the platoon climbed out from their holes, over which they had carefully placed boughs of trees to keep reconnoitering airplanes from seeing the freshly dug dirt.

Garrett's helmet felt as if it were about to come off. It wobbled from one side to the other. His face was frozen, and when he wanted to speak out he felt that he could not because the muscles that controlled his mouth refused to respond. At first he was intensely aware of his legs, but, surging along with the rest of the platoon, he soon forgot them.

Three Germans were rising up in front of him. "Don't those queer little caps of theirs look funny?" he thought, and, from the hip, he fired his automatic rifle at them. One fell and the others lifted their hands in the air and bellowed: "Kamerad! Kamerad!"[18] Garrett passed by them,

---

[18] Loose translation: Mate; in other words, I surrender.

unheeding. More Germans. The woods were filled with Germans. But the rest of them wore heavy steel helmets that covered their foreheads and ears.

"You dirty bastards!" Garrett heard someone scream.

By God, he wouldn't have any liquid fire poured on him. "Sullivan!" he called. But Sullivan, his loader, was not there. Garrett's last clip had been emptied of shells. There were no more in his musette bag. It wasn't possible! Sullivan must be some place near, ready to give him more clips. But no! He threw his rifle away in disgust. A few yards farther he saw the back of an olive-drab uniform and in one of the hands that was connected to the uniform was clutched a rifle. Garrett snatched the rifle, unbuckled the cartridge-belt from the uniform, and hurried blindly on.

A deep ravine was in front of him. He half jumped, half stumbled acrossed it, and found himself once more in a wheat-field. There was no one in sight. He scrambled back over the ravine and through the woods again, frightened but defiant. Wherever he looked, as he went back through the woods, men were lying. Some of them lay quite still. Others moaned and cried alternately. But Garrett paid no heed. He was still hurrying on, his head up and his nostrils wide, when someone called: "Here, Garrett, get busy and round up some of these Squareheads." It was Sergeant Powell.

Garrett felt as if he had been struck in the stomach with a brick. He laughed nervously. "Sure."
Nine Germans stood together with their hands raised high above their heads. Their knees were shaking badly and they looked first to one side and then to the other. Docile sheep, he led them back to the village where he turned them over to a Reserve Regiment.

On the way back to join his platoon he met a man who looked familiar. "Say, fellow, don't you belong to A Company, of the Fifth?"

The man turned. "I did," he said. "I don't believe there is any more A Company."

"What do you mean?"

"Why, we attacked this morning through an open space in the woods," the man told him.

"And they're all dead? Fellah, I've got a cousin in that outfit. Show me where they went over."

They walked back to the clearing together. Men were lying around in all manner of postures, and much more thickly than the men in the woods.

"What was your cousin's name, buddy?"

"Ford, Jerome Ford," Garrett jerked out. "He was a tall, dark-haired fellow, about nineteen?"

"Nope. Might have seen him, but I don't remember his name."

Garrett covered the entire field, stopping closely to peer into the face of each of the men who was not a German soldier. As he was turning away from a man who was lying upon his back, his arms and legs stretched wide, and over whom he had stood longer than usual because the face reminded him somewhat of his cousin, the man's eyelids partly opened, and in a voice in which there was little strength, called: "Soldier! Oh, soldier! Don't let that damned Squarehead get me. Don't leave me alone with him. He'll kill me."

"No, he won't, buddy. He's all right." Garrett spoke reassuringly. For a moment he could not think whom the man was speaking of, but then he recollected that a German Red Cross attendant had been busy in the field, binding the wounds of the soldiers. Garrett looked around and saw the attendant a few yards off. He beckoned to him, and tried to illustrate by motions that he wanted the soldier carried back to the first-aid station.

The German came over, lowered his head to the soldier's chest. "Nein. Caput."[19] He pointed to a rust-colored spot on the soldier's tunic over the heart. While Garrett was standing there, wondering what to do, the soldier's eyelids fluttered, he breathed once and deeply - and died.

Garrett gave up hope of finding his cousin. He had either been taken prisoner, and that was not at all likely, or else he had been sent back wounded, he thought.

Garrett tramped back through the thick woods that suddenly had become quiet. The rays of the noonday sun were filtering through the boughs of the trees, seeking out the now inanimate bodies, which would soon turn black and bloat out of shape under the intense heat. Before him, on a knoll of green, was a pile of heavy boulders, and, peeping through a crevice, stuck the nose of a Maxim. Climbing the knoll to the right, he looked into the machine-gun nest. Three bodies, motionless as the rocks themselves, were stretched at length. One had fallen face forward, an arm thrown over the stock of the weapon. His back, that swelled under the gray coat, was turned reproachfully toward the sky. Another was sprawled supine, his hands and legs frozen in a gesture of complete negation. His chin had fallen heavily on his breast and upon his head his small trench cap was tilted forward at a rakish angle. The other man's face was a clot of blood. Death, camera-like, had caught and held him fast, his body supported by the rocks, his face like a battered sunflower in the evening.

Garrett stooped over and gently drew the Maxim away from the man who had been firing it when he had been killed. Shouldering it, and

---

[19] Loose translation: No. Gone.

carrying an extra belt of cartridges and the water-cooler, he left the knoll and walked toward the ravine. The spectacle that he had just witnessed left very little impression upon him.

The platoon was gathered closely together in the ravine. The ravine was deep and wide, and every so often passage along it was obstructed by a huge stone over which the men would have to climb. Evidently, a few days before, the French soldiers had used the ravine as a trench from which to conceal themselves while they fought against the onslaught of the enemy. Little holes had been dug in the side of the ravine nearest to the field in which men could throw themselves to be protected from the bursting shell casings and shrapnel. As he approached, three of the men were scuffing dirt over the body of a dead French soldier who had fallen near one of the small burrows in the ravine.

Sergeant Powell was pacing along the ravine, pulling at the ends of his pointed mustache. Lieutenant Harris, chewing speculatively at a sprig of wheat, and Sergeant Walker were seated on the ground, apparently immersed in a discussion.

Sergeant Powell walked over to them.

"This is damned foolishness," he called. "Before very long there are going to be so many shells flying into this place that you won't be able to count them. And where will we be? In hell, if we loaf around here much longer."

Lieutenant Harris rubbed with the palm of his hand the stubble on his pallid face. "If I knew how much longer we were to be here, Powell, I would have had the men digging in long ago."

The Company Commander broke through the edge of the woods, and stood on the edge of the ravine. "Lieutenant Harris. I want six of your men right away."

"Yes, sir," Harris answered. "You, Garrett; you, Parker; you, Perry; you, Sullivan; you, Rogers, and Foster. Follow Captain Anderson."

Joined by details from the three other platoons, the men followed along through the woods again and out into a field which was very near to the place where Garrett had searched for his cousin that morning.

"Have all of you men your rifles loaded?"

They responded in the affirmative.

"Well," Captain Anderson hesitated, "you see that little bunch of woods over there? There's a number of Germans there and we're going after them."

Swishing through the heavy wheat, the men now advanced in skirmish order. They were very cautious and, although the sun was making a glaring light and they were directly in an open field, they walked as though they were sneaking toward the enemy. Captain Anderson, forgetting his impressive dignity, slunk along, one shoulder low and his hand grasping the middle a rifle. His eyes were narrowed as if he were registering extreme wariness, for the motion-pictures. As gently and softly as wading through heavy grass permitted, Captain Anderson placed one foot after the other. His manner infected the men. One by one they adopted the crouching attitude, ready to spring upon their unsuspecting prey. They could almost be seen to flex the muscles in the calves of their legs and in their upper arms, rising majestically on their toes when they walked, instead of using the customary flat-footed form of perambulation.

Captain Anderson, abandoning his duties as instructor of English at the Texas college, had learned modern warfare from the books supplied by the nearest officers' training camp. He had learned how to order men about and that he was an officer and a gentleman. But yet he felt a slight interest in the men of his command. In the officers' training-school and in the course of the practice skirmishes through which he had been, he had learned that the way in which an attack was made by a small party moving forward in full daylight was by running forward in spurts until the objective had been reached.

Being a professor of English, and especially a professor of English in Texas, he sentimentalized the attack. How much finer it was to attack as General Sam Houston attacked; to march steadfastly upon the enemy and make them surrender at the point of a sword or a bowie-knife. The only rift came in his realization that he had no sword, not even a bowie-knife.

When the party was still several yards from the edge of the woods, a mass of Germans, outnumbering them twice, emerged with their hands held high in the air and, in their eagerness to surrender, almost twittering: "Kamerad."

The Captain's disappointment at not being able to make another attack worthy of a Texan was soon lost in his exultant emotion at the thought of the number of prisoners he had captured. Selecting one of the men to go with him, he herded the prisoners back to the Regimental Headquarters, where he proudly delivered them to another officer.

CHAPTER TWELVE

In the ravine Garrett was busy trying to place his Maxim in a position from which it would sweep a portion of the field. He had succeeded in making it remain upright on its haunches, and was now experimenting with it in various positions, so that he could swing it back and forth as he fired, and cover the maximum of ground. The water-cooler had been set at its side and the long rubber hose was attached to the machine-gun. A belt filled with cartridges was inserted in the chamber, and the affair was ready to be fired.

"'At's some gun you got there, Garrett, old boy. What do you 'spect to do with it? You don't aim to kill nobody, do you?" Morrow had recovered and was in good humor. As he talked, a black stubble of beard that grew grotesquely on the chin of his elf-like face rose and fell.

"No, Morrow. I'm just keepin' it for a souvenir."

"Hell, y'ain't got no souvenir. Lookit, Garrett." He produced a small pearl-handled pistol. "Got this offen one of them Dutchmen.[20] Lookit here." He placed his hand in his blouse and brought out a pair of field glasses. "Got this from another one. Now all I want to do is to git wounded and I'll take these babies back and sell 'em for beaucoup francs to them S.O.S. birds."[21]

---

[20] German.
[21] Battalion Hospital.

"Don't talk about getting wounded, Morrow," Walker requested. "It's bad luck. Remember what Phillips said the other night?"

"Naw, how'd I know what Phillips said? He didn't say nothin' to me."

"He said that he'd either win a decoration or get killed."

"I don't care if he did. I want a bon-bless-ey[22] so I can git outta this damn hole."

"Say, Garrett," Rogers called, "you'd better take down that confounded gun. The Boche will see it and then we'll all get killed."

"Oh, they won't see it."

"You can't tell. One of their aviators is liable to come over here any time."

"Tyah tyah tyah tyah, you talk like you come from where they have possums for yard dogs, Rogers," Morrow sneered. "Garrett, let's you and me go out salvagin'. There's a lot of salmon and stuff in some of them boys' packs that'll never want it no more."

"You mean some of the fellows that have been killed?" Garrett asked. "I don't like to do that. It seems too ghoulish."

"I don't cah what it seems like. I'm hawngry. Let's go."

"Maybe Harris'll stop us."

"Naw, he won't. He's too damned scared to git out of his hole."

They climbed out of the ravine and started back through the woods.

---

[22] Loose translation: Good blessing (in other words, orders back home).

"Garrett! Be damned! Lookit that!"

"Where, where? What is it?"

"Look!" Morrow pointed his finger toward a large tree. Its knees on the ground and its forehead pressed stiffly against the bark of the tree, a body kneeled.

"Let's go back."

"Naw, I wanta git some of that salmon."

It was easy enough without touching the bodies to collect armfuls of the tinned fish from the packs of the dead men. Soon they had all they could carry. Besides the salmon, Morrow had collected several razors and a can of talcum.

They had but reached the ravine when the bottom seemed to drop from the sky, dumping a deluge of shells. For a moment the men were stunned by the fierceness of the bombardment. Garrett and Morrow emptied their arms of the cans and dived for a burrow, reaching it simultaneously. Another flock of shells struck in and around the ravine. It was not until after they had exploded that the report of their departure was heard.

"Oh-o, Garrett, can't you get in a little closer and give me some room," Morrow yelled. "Them's the whizz-bangs they've been tellin' us about."

The shells, with their terrific "bzzz—BANG, bzzz—BANG" poured in upon the men.

"Stretcher bearer on the left!" someone screamed above the racket. The plea went unheeded.

"God damn it, there's a man half killed up there. Stretcher bearer on the le-f-f-t."

"I didn't know there was anybody fool enough to yell for one of them lousy stretcher bearers. Garrett, le's you and me go up."

While the shells fell and burst directly in front of him, behind him, and on each side, a huge fellow whose proportions made him an easy target walked conscientiously along the ravine. In his hand was a bag containing first-aid implements, and there was a red cross on his arm. As he went past Garrett he looked like a doting father who felt the necessity forcibly to reprimand a child. A few minutes later Garrett saw him, with the wounded man thrown over his shoulder as if he were a bag of salt, making his way along the ravine and through the woods to the dressing station.

Bang - CRASH. The ravine reverberated from the explosion. Another volley had been hurled into it.

"Stretcher bearer on the left. Stretcher bearer on the left," someone called. From time to time the cry was repeated, each time less hopefully, more stridently.

Fiercely whining, a shell bore down upon the ground under which Garrett and Morrow were crouched. It landed softly. They waited, breathless, for it to burst. Garrett was convulsed. Oh, if only it would explode and end the suspense. Garrett found himself wanting the shell to burst, imploring it!

The smoke in the air was stifling them, burning out their lungs. Their eyes were shot with blood, and tears streamed unceasingly down their cheeks. Their throats felt as if they had swallowed handfuls of fine dust.

"I'll choke, I'll die," Garrett thought with every breath. He felt for his mask, knocked off his helmet, and adjusted the mask to his head. Frenzied, he bit his teeth into the hard-rubber mouthpiece, and breathed deeply. Oh, what a relief; the picrine[23] could not penetrate the chemicals of the mask! He breathed again; gulped, rather. Immediately his throat and lungs were on fire. The mask was more of a hindrance than a help.

Incomprehensibly, the bombardment stopped.

Men ran from their burrows and clambered over the ravine in an effort to escape the blinding, choking smoke.

"Stop, men," Lieutenant Harris called hoarsely. "Come back here and be ready to stand off an attack."

Reluctantly they returned and placed themselves in a position from which they could fire across the field. Garrett drew out his canteen. It was empty.

"Water, got any water, Morrow?"

"No, jist drained the last drop."

Garrett walked down the ravine. "Anybody got any water to spare?"

No one had. No one had any water. He walked back beside Morrow. As he approached, Morrow called: "Oh, Garrett, you'd better go over and ask them Dutchmen for another gun. One of their shells swiped that pretty one you had up here."

The Maxim which Garrett had diligently striven to get into shape was gone - where, no one knew.

---

[23] Poisonous gas.

"I don't care. If they come over now I wouldn't have strength enough to pull a trigger." He dropped down.

Fearfully, the men waited for the attack. It grew dark, but none came. Out in the field a malnourished cow slowly moved across the broken ground. In the dusk Lieutenant Harris was stumbling along the ravine, calling for volunteers to go on a water detail.

From one of the holes Parker's voice croaked: "I'll go, Lieutenant. I'll go." He sounded like a bullfrog.

"I'll go, too; be glad to," Garrett offered.

"God, me too," complemented Morrow.

"I only want two men. Morrow, you stay here. All right, Garrett and Parker, collect up the canteens and then I'll tell you where to go."

"Je's, these canteens make a lot of noise. The Squareheads can hear us for a mile. Hadn't we better put something around them?" Garrett asked Lieutenant Harris.

"Yes, have the men unhook their canteen covers and put them on. Now be careful when you go, for the German lines are only a few hundred yards. You follow this ravine until you come to a place where it splits. Take the one to the right. It leads into a little town where there's a pump."

CHAPTER THIRTEEN

Garrett and Parker started off, feeling their way over the huge boulders that lay in the ravine. When they were no more than a hundred yards from the platoon, a shell severed the air over their heads and burst in the field to their right. They fell flat on their faces. After the shell had exploded they got up and started again. Another shell burst ten yards in front of them. They ran forward again, the canteens jangling over their shoulders. This time the shell burst just to their left, throwing up a mass of dirt which showered down on them.

"Good-by, canteens; I'm goin' to throw mine away and run," said Parker.

"You do and we die of thirst. Come on, it's not far now."

They hurried blindly on. Another shell screeched over their heads and struck the edge of the ravine to their right. They were violently thrown against the opposite side.

"I sure do admire that boy's aim. Let's go, Garrett."

Abruptly the ravine shallowed out and they found themselves running for the village, their bodies wholly exposed. As they approached, a door in one of the buildings of the badly battered town was thrown open and a voice called: "Here you are, fellows. Come in this way."

"Hell, if you think you had it hard, you ought to have been with us."

Garrett and Parker, resting after they had filled the canteens with water from a creaky pump in the village square, were seated in a room of the building through which they had entered the town. At the window near the door a thin-snouted Hotchkiss machine-gun was pointed out over the field. Beside it, his head lying against the saddle, a man was reclining. It was he who had spoken.

"Think of carrying one of these guns over your shoulder and walking through heavy rifle fire the whole length of that field! Pretty tough. Pretty tough."

"Oh, forget about it; it'd a been worse if you'd a been killed."

"I don't know so much about that!"

"And when we got in this town. Boy, we sure did clump them Dutchmen over the head! Firin' out of the windows, they were, and us comin' in plain sight. But we knocked 'em for a gool, a cock-eyed gool. I thought them God-damned Squareheads could fight." He chuckled and stretched his body. "But you oughta seen 'em run when we swarmed in here."

"I guess they fought well enough to knock off most of us," stated one of his buddies.

Garrett shuffled his feet restlessly. "Guess we'd better be gettin' back, Parker."

It had grown quite dark and along the lines of restless men white rockets were fired, to flare for a moment, covering a part of the ground with an intense brightness and then expiring on the ground with a short hiss.

The platoon was not in sight when they returned to the mouth of the ravine. But as the clanking of their canteens was heard, men hurried from their burrows and surrounded Garrett and Parker.

"Here, give me mine."

"Mine's the one with the dent in the side, Parker."

"That's not my canteen. Here, let me find it."

"Git the hell away from here or you'll never git anything to drink. Who the devil went after this water, anyway?"

Sergeant Walker stood in the background, much to the surprise of Garrett, who had expected him to rush forward demanding that he be given his canteen first of all. The canteens were passed out and Walker's was the next to the last one.

"Thank you, Garrett," said Walker warmly.

"Go easy on that water now; we can't go running to that town every five minutes, you men," Sergeant Powell called.

Along the ravine the water gurgled from the canteens into the mouths of the men. Their most pressing want satisfied, their thoughts soon turned to the matter of food, which they had been without for two days, save for the cans of salmon which Garrett and Morrow had salvaged from the dead men's packs. After expressing among themselves their desire for food they raised their voices and began to lament: "What makes the wildcats wild?"

"Because they're hungry."

"Why are they hungry?"

"Because there ain't no chow."

"Why ain't they got no chow?"

"Because they ain't got nobody to look out for them."

"Pipe down, up there," scolded Lieutenant Harris. "If the ration detail don't come along pretty soon, we'll send one of our own after the chow."

Hours of quiet passed, while the men silently lay in their burrows in the ravine, listening to the cheerful chirp of the crickets, and trying to relax their nerves which had been tautened almost to breaking by the terrific barrage of the early afternoon.

"Je's, I wish we had some more of that salmon, Morrow. We were crazy to give it all away."

"No, we wasn't. These mamma's boys'd starve to death if somebody didn't pr'vide for 'em."

While they were talking, Sergeant Walker, stealing along the ravine, came to their burrow: "Here's some Argentina beef that you fellows can have some of. I got three cans of it."

It was a little blue can, and when Morrow lifted a piece of it to his mouth he shuddered. "Smells like somep'n you've stepped in. Mah guts can't do that stuff."

"Yes, they can," Walker encouraged. "It's not half bad if you don't breathe while you're chewing. I've been eating it all day."

Morrow, holding his nostrils together, gulped down a handful of the evil-smelling food. "That's not so bad, Garrett. Try some of it."

He passed the can over to Garrett.

CHAPTER FOURTEEN

In the early morning the German lines were represented by a black strip of woods, some five hundred yards in the distance, that looked like a narrow piece of jet-black lace through the gray dawn. To the men on watch it was inconceivable that such a calm, almost sketched scene existed so near to them. The brain-piercing explosions of the shells still remembered, the calmness of the surroundings was unreal. Quiet belonged to another world.

Day broke fully. From above, the hot sun beat cruelly upon the earth. The helmets of the men were like hot frying-pans. Sweat soaked through the padding and ran down the men's faces in tiny, dirty rivulets. Their skin, beneath their woolen shirts and breeches, itched unbearably. At the knees, where the breeches tightly fitted, the shell powder had soaked through and was biting the flesh.

There was a sameness about the expressions on the men's faces. As yet it was barely perceptible. The mouths had set in certain rigid lines. The lids of the eyes were narrowed, and beneath them the pupils reflected only a dull apathy. Of each man the shoulders sagged as if bowed down with a dreadful weight.

Garrett lay against the sloping wall of the ravine, his head peeping over, watching an airplane circle lazily above. The drone of its engine was like some enormous bluebottle fly. It was soothing. A slight breeze rippled the wheat. "Ah," he breathed. But on the breeze was carried a stomach-turning stench. It was sweet and putrid and seemed to take substance around the nostrils. As the heat of the day grew more, the odor strengthened until Garrett felt as if he were submerged in it up to his eyes.

As the sun glided out of sight the odor became less evident, until at last, as the shadows were thrown full length, it ceased entirely to be.

Lieutenant Harris made his way along the ravine. "Where's Sergeant Walker?"

Walker poked his pallid face out of his burrow.

"Yes, sir?"

"Oh, there you are, Walker. Pick out four men to go after rations. Right after dark."

"Shall I go along in charge?"

"Go if you want to. Powell and I can take care of things all right."

The ration party tracked through the thick woods, purpled with late evening. Trees stretched gaunt arms in awkward gestures toward the somber-colored sky, through which lights gaily winked and danced. Under foot were objects over which they tried to step without touching. Now and then a foot would strike a dead man's pack or his body, and someone would draw back, mutter "Damn," feeling as if he had committed sacrilege. Branches of trees, half torn from the trunks by shell explosion, barred their way. On they walked, their hands flung out in front of them, and keeping as closely to each other as was possible. Passing one place in the woods Walker thought: "Here's where Sanders got killed."

They went on farther. An open space in the woods reminded him that it was there that Phillips received three machine-gun bullets through his head. "He's probably rotten by this time." Walker shivered to his marrow. It seemed hours before they got out of the woods and into the field through which a small dusty road ran toward the village where they had first gone into action.

In outline the buildings, worn down by heavy shell fire, clung to each other for moral encouragement. They looked so tightly clustered in their common misery suffered by devastation.

A shell, like the flash of lightning, hurtled over and resounded as does that kind of lightning after which one says: "That struck somewhere, all right."

The village was being used as the supply station for the regiment. Inside the shattered houses and barns the field kitchens had been drawn; in the dim light made by candles the Mess Sergeant was the center of a group of unwashed louts dressed in greasy blue denim.

"Say, Butler, where's our chow?"

"Been sellin' another quarter of beef to the Frogs again?"

"Don't you let us catch you at any o' them fancy tricks."

Butler was a small, shifty-looking person. It had been found out by the platoon that he had once sold the company axe to a Frenchman for a gallon of vin rouge, and since that time he had always been suspected of making away with the Company's rations.

"How do you boys expect to git any chow if you don't come after it? The chow was here, but you wasn't."

"You think we can fight Germans and run back here after chow, too?" The men were belligerent.

"Of course he does. These damned yellah grease balls ain't got any sense."

"Yellow? I like that. Jist because you guys are up there at the front that ain't no sign there ain't other places jist as dangerous."

The squabble would have gone on indefinitely had not the arrival of a flock of shells ended it then.

Butler had thrown himself under the field kitchen, where he arrived at the same time his assistant did.

The rations party had remained standing. "Get up, Butler," Walker commanded, "and get our chow."

There was coffee, boiled potatoes, boiled beef and white bread. Placing a stick through the handles of the coffee container, Walker and another man led the way. One man carried the bread and the other two brought the potatoes and meat.

They walked along the road to the woods without an adventure. Through the woods they made their way without a mishap until they arrived at a clearing. Then, for some reason, a salvo of shells were fired which struck with the wild shriek of some lost soul. After the shell had exploded, the man with the bread could be seen gathering up the loaves from where they had rolled when he threw himself on the ground. The others had remained standing for fear they would spill the food.

"Oh, Garrett. Garrett, the ration party's come."

Morrow shook Garrett from his slumber.

"What . . . The ration party? Whatta they got?"

"That's jis' what I'm goin' to see. Hurry up or the rest of these hogs'll eat it all up on us."

They walked quickly toward the place where a queue of men had formed.

"Hurry up, you guys. Bring your canteen cups."

It was a glorious moment.

"Is it hot?" asked Garrett.

"Hot as blazes."

"Hold me, Morrow, I'm faintin' with joy. Coffee, hot! And milk and sugar in it."

They sat around and munched their food and drank their coffee. Under the feeling of warmth in their stomachs many of the men relaxed and their thoughts became once again normal.

CHAPTER FIFTEEN

The platoon had grown used to the late afternoon bombardment that beat and slashed at them every day. The shells driving at them with a white fury were accepted as a part of the whole stunning, disagreeable duty of the front line. As their durance in the ravine lengthened they were able even to comment upon the fierceness or the comparative mildness of the attack.

In his burrow Sergeant Powell, his blouse and undershirt lying by his side, was exploring with his right hand a place beneath his left shoulder-blade that had begun to pain. His fingers felt a swollen, hurting lump. As he pressed on it, a pain like being prodded in a nerve with a needle shot through him.

Lieutenant Harris, from a burrow nearby, leaned out.

"What's the matter, Powell? Looking for cooties?"

"No, there's something the matter with my shoulder. It's swelled."

"Let's see . . . Hell, man, you'd better go back to the dressing station. You've been hit."

"Take your knife and see if you can get it out."

"What do you think I am, a surgeon? You report to the first-aid station and let them send you to the hospital. I don't want any men to come down with gangrene."

Powell, reluctant, departed alone, his small reddish mustache still smartly waxed, his puttees neatly rolled, his helmet set jauntily on his head.

In the early morning light the outlines of the objects in front of the ravine were crisply apparent. The strands of barbed wire were blackly filigreed against the opaque light of the horizon. An aluminum moon hung waveringly in the sky. The stalks of wheat stood stiffly erect, their yellowness merging in the distance with the shadowy green of the trees. On the breath of the morning wind was carried the sickening smell of decayed cadavers. To the left and to the right unbroken lines of infinite length lay huddled in holes, the guardians of their snoring hours seeing without variation the same sight. For the sector which the platoon was holding the night had not been quiet. Eyes, though worn with constant straining to pierce the shadows, had seen the wheat tops moving; and ears, the drums battered by the explosion of striking shells, had still heard the rustling among the stalks. So rifles, venomous and catlike, had spit shots of fire into the dark.

As the sun rose, the heat growing more intense, the nauseating smell from the corpses in the field seemed to coat all objects in one's line of vision with a sticky green. Even the tops of wheat, standing stiffly in the field looked as if they were covered with a fetid substance.

Occasionally, as the day advanced, a man would labor over the opening of a can of Argentina beef with the point of his bayonet. And then the contents would be exposed, green and sepulchrally white, the odor mingling and not quite immersed in the odor of decaying human flesh.

Laboring over the small blue can, sweat poured down their chests, the streams dislodging particles of dirt and sweeping them down their bodies.

The air was dead. The sky was suspended not high above the earth. The odors had ceased to move; they were massive, grotesquely shaped objects fastly rooted to the earth. The silence was elephantine.

And somewhere in the everlasting silence a frightened, hurt, bewildered voice broke tentatively forth: "Landsmann. Oh, Landsmann! Kamerad. Hilfen Sie mich."

Garrett and Morrow, their heads peering over the crest of the ravine, started, then listened, their ears like terriers'.

"Mein Gott. Ich bin gewundet. O-o-o G-o-tt." The voice floated through the heavy stillness.

Morrow put the butt of his rifle to his shoulder. "Watch out; it's one of their damned tricks."

"Put down your gun, you fool. Nobody could fake a voice like that."

While they were talking the voice once again reached them. In the stillness it seemed as if it were at their sides. "Landsmann, Landsmann, hilf mich bitte."

"The poor fellow must be half dead. Poor Kruger![24] Oh, Edwards, there's a wounded Squarehead out in front here. Talk to him, will you?"

A bleached but eager-faced Edwards came out of his burrow and commenced to talk in German to the wounded man.

"What does he say, Edwards? What does he say?" A group had gathered around the scene.

---

[24] A slang term for a German soldier.

"He says some of you guys shot him in the guts and that he's pretty bad off."

"Well, let's go out and git him. We can't let him lie there all day."

"Is he all right, Edwards? I mean is he a good guy?"

"How the hell do I know? He sounds all right."

"Edwards." Morrow insinuated himself closer. "Edwards, let's you and me go git him? Huh?"

They went.

The German had to be moved very carefully. Directly above the wide leather belt that he wore around the waist the gray uniform was soaked with blood. Morrow and Edwards carried him from the field and lowered him to the bottom of the ravine.

"Now what do you think of the Kaiser, you damn Squarehead?"

"Bet, by God, he wishes he'd stayed home drinkin' beer."

"Hell, these Dutchmen git beer right in the trenches." The speaker passed his tongue over his dry lips.

"Shut up. Can't you let the poor devil alone? He probably hates the Kaiser as much as the rest of us."

The wounded German raised himself on his shoulder, gasping with pain. "Kaiser. Gottverdammt." He fell back exhausted.

The stretcher bearers who had been sent for arrived and placed him on a stretcher. They started to carry him to the dressing station.

"Wait a minute there, buddy." A muddy, wizened-face soldier, advancing with an open razor in his hand, snipped a button from the German's tunic. "That, there goes home to my gal."

The platoon had been subjected to heavy bombardment, since two weeks earlier they had occupied the ravine, but upon this particular afternoon there was a force, a spitefulness, an overwhelming, dull, sickening insistence to the dropping, exploding shells that made each one of the men feel that, as any of them would have expressed it, "one of them seabags[25] has got my name marked on it in big letters."

The shells hammered over, shaking the sides of the ravine as they broke and sending particles of flying steel through the air and ripping into the ground. Men called for stretcher bearers until there were no more stretcher bearers, and, as it seemed, as if there were no more men to call. And meanwhile the thick, pungent smoke from the exploding shells was filling up the ravine and seeking out the throats and eyes of the men, to blind and choke them. Before it was over there were men, ostrich-like, with their heads in their burrows as far as they could get them. Many of them were blubbering, not so much from fright as from nerves that had broken under the insistent battering of the shells. But when it ended they were ready at the call to standby to repel an enemy of any size.

It was felt certain that this time there would be an attack by the Germans to regain the woods from which they had been driven. The men were working the bolts of their rifles, or trying to check the tears that flowed from their eyes, inflamed by the heavy smoke. But while they were making ready to stand off the attack the Company Commander sent a runner to Lieutenant Harris, telling him that the platoon would be relieved for the night by other men, and that they were to return farther back in the woods and rest in case there was no attack.

---

[25] Cadaver bag.

Gasping and choking, the platoon made its way out of the ravine and up the hill. Exhausted, they dropped into the holes, slightly deeper than their own, that the relieving men had occupied. The Captain, with his orderly and his runners in holes around him, was lying back on the ground, peacefully smoking a cigarette.

The attack which the officers had anticipated failed to be made. The sun withdrew from the scene and a pale gold moon took its place, stars peeped out like eyes, and the air became thin and chilly. The men were beginning to feel that they were to enjoy a night's sleep.

Far off a faint whining began. Nearer and nearer it came, growing louder and awe-inspiring. It was as if some high priest of the elements were working himself into a frenzy before hurling an incantation at his supplicants. It grew to a snarl, a bitter snarl full of hate, and it seemed as if the high priest had bared his teeth, which were long, narrow, and sharply pointed. The tree limbs bowed in fright, and against the dull-blue sky the leaves turned under, curling themselves up. Like a hurricane the shells descended, and with terrific noise they threw out splashes of reds and yellows, in the light of which the trees seemed to cringe.

"We're in for it," thought Garrett, trying to coordinate his jangling nerves. He sought more closely to press his body against the clayey side of his burrow. Sharply and frighteningly another salvo of shells struck and burst in the little patch of woods. Garrett bit at the leather strap of his helmet.

The tree limbs crackled and falling branches fell hesitatingly through the foliage to the ground. Other shells burst. "Oh, my God, I'm hit!" someone cried. And before he had ended his words another group of shells pounded over. Garrett's spine felt bare with scorpions parading along the flesh. *I won't get killed. I can't get killed. I've got too much to live for*, he thought, as the bursting shells continued and pieces of their steel casing ripped past and viciously over him. *Oh, God, don't let me die.* The shells mocked him. *Shall I pray? What shall I say? Oh, it wouldn't do any good!* But he formulated an incoherent prayer between interruptions of his fancying that among the trees was a huge black animal with fiery eyes and hoofs of brimstone that were kicking and prancing all over the woods. The animal's head was above the trees, and it snapped at their limbs with its long, punishing jaws. Garrett felt as if his eyes would pop from his head and that his temples would split. The animal's hoofs kicked nearer him, and he closed his eyes and twisted his neck in fear. Red, purple, white lights danced before his eyes. He turned round to face the monster, forcing a grin over his stiff face. Then he began to cry and then . . . blackness, all was blackness.

The morning sun sent wavering rays through the boughs of the trees, and exposed the white stumps whose tops had been blown to the earth by exploding shells. Tree limbs, with ghastly butts, lay dead-still on the thick, calm grass. Steel helmets, spattered with blood, were now and then encountered on the ground. On the space where the Captain had been lying there was a blood-soaked shoe and a helmet, turned bottom up, and neatly holding a mess of brains. Nearby lay a gas-mask which would never again be used. And near it the sleeve of a coat.

Garrett awakened and cautiously sat up, his head peeping over the top of his burrow. Close enough to be touched - a body, the legs spread wide, the chin raised high, and the chest slightly puffed, offered its belly to the sun. Garrett stiffly got out and looked at the body. "By God, they did come close all right," he breathed.

Garrett walked over to the helmet. Like an inexperienced surgeon prodding a wound, he touched at the helmet, finally discovering on the leather cover of the padding the initials "CAPT. ANDERSON." As he straightened he felt a deep pity, a great sorrow. "I used to cuss him a lot and he was an awrful bonehead, but he was a pretty good fellow."

Weighted down by two large food containers, four men made their way, stumbling and cursing, into the patch of woods. Seeing no one but Garrett, one angrily called: "Hey, you guys, don't you want no chow?"

Out of nowhere a group of perhaps twenty-five men gathered around the pails of food.

"All right, you guys, snap it up. We can't wait here all day. Quit fingerin' your noses and grab your mess kits."

Another man, resting from carrying the heavy stuff, started forth:

> Oh, the infantry and the cavalry
> And the dirty engineers,
> They couldn't lick the doughboys
> In a hundred thousand years.

Morrow looked at him sourly. "You all wouldn't be singin' that if you'd of been with us las' night. You musta been hidin' in some dugout eatin' up our rations."

"Who?" The man broke off, indignant.

"Who? Who?" mocked Morrow. "You ain't no owl. Your feet don't fit no limb."

"Who do you mean?" - incensed.

"Oh, gwahn."

With their canteen cups the men dipped eagerly into the thick, brown, greasy fluid.

"God, an' it's hot, too."

But for the most part they were silent. One man tasted of the concoction in the other receptacle. He began to retch horribly.

Usually, the early afternoon was the period of the day's recreation for the men in the ravine, an hour more favorable to their personal pursuits. Between the time when an attack might be expected and the diurnal four-o'clock German bombardment, the moment gave the platoon a chance once more to assume their normal existence. At such a time the guardians of the ravine would emerge from their burrows and, under the shade of an overhanging tree, try to recollect their thoughts.

It was now such a time, and Sergeant Walker was sitting cross-legged in the ravine, assaulting with the point of his bayonet a can of Argentina beef. Events of late had left him shaken. He had entered the trenches with a handicap; he believed that he was a crusader reincarnate, engaged in the holy service of saving religion, morality, purity, and civilization from the barbaric hand of that nation whose people he referred to as Huns. He had enlisted because he was of draft age and would be unqualified to dodge the call of Congress, requesting him to join the selected army of the United States of America. Had possessed no mother, nor a wife and child, he would as gladly have fought the Hun from an office desk in Kenosha.

He had pierced the cover of the foul beef when a messenger from battalion headquarters parted the trees near Walker and dropped in the ravine, Seeing Walker, he spoke: "Is this the Third Platoon?"

"It is, you know." Walker had picked up the postscript to his sentence from a man of many enlistments and whom he tried in many ways to emulate.

"You one of the non-coms?"

"Yes," Walker answered pleasantly.

"Well." The messenger reached in the leather saddlebag suspended from his shoulders. "Got some mail for the Third Platoon. You take it?"

"Bet I will." Walker fairly grabbed at the package of letters, so eager he was to see if it contained one for him. Yes, there it was. The one he had expected, waited for these many days.

"Thompson!" he called. "Thompson, do you want to give out the mail?"

Thompson hurried forward, got the package, and ran to the middle of the ravine, calling: "Mail Call!! Mail Call!! Third Platoon!!"

CHAPTER SIXTEEN

The envelope which Walker fondly and carefully opened was different from the other letters in the package. On it the stamp had been glued at an angle which, to many young men and women, meant I love you. The stationery was lavender and a reminiscent odor of sachet was on it. The writing was cramped and affectedly school-girlish. Walker unfolded the sheet of lavender paper.

> *Dear Douglas,*
> *You poor dear boy! How you must be suffering over there in those horrid trenches. And how brave of you to be so joking about it. But we know how badly the conditions really are. The papers keep reporting the frightfulness of those Huns, and I pray each night that you won't be taken prisoner and be treated as some of our poor boys have been treated. The other day Mrs. Prescott told me the most awful story of what the Huns were doing to our prisoner boys. Oh, Douglas, it was so awful that I cannot repeat it. I ought not to even think of it. But I know that my Douglas is too brave to let himself be taken prisoner.*
>
> *Four of your letters came today. I sent you a box two weeks ago. I wonder if you got it. I put in a cap that I had knitted especially for you, and six big bars of chocolate. You must have plenty of cigarettes. Both Helene Mason and I have subscribed to oodles of soldiers' tobacco funds. You know, you pay a quarter and get a box of cigarettes and tobacco. You can write whosever name on it that you want to and it will be sent to him. So of course I made Helene write yours. I know that you used to*

not smoke cigarettes, but the papers say that now that all the boys over there are smoking them and of course you would be doing what the rest of the boys are. Remember, I didn't use to like to see boys smoke. But I am willing to sacrifice a mere prejudice for so great a cause as you boys are fighting for. And then Rector Tyson, of the First M. E., said from the pulpit the other Sunday that he thought it was all right for the boys over there to smoke. He is so broad-minded!

Douglas dear, this war will never end. You have been over there so long. Almost a year, and I keep thinking about John Ryder. He has a big farm now and is raising the food that the government most needs, and says that you will never come back. Would you forgive me if I did, Douglas? I mean, became Mrs. John R. Ryder? You better hurry or I will.

*Your loving
Ellen*

Hope was burned to a white crisp in his intense disappointment. It left him feeling cold and as if a large hole had been burned in his side. His eyes were blinded and weak as if by a sudden glare. *Oh, damn. Oh, damn.* He crushed the letter in the palm of his hand, making it a paper wad. Feverishly he unfolded the letter, spreading out the wrinkles. Ellen danced before him, a fiend with golden hair, an angel who had a forked tongue. She didn't care, she never cared. But she did, a voice informed him, rationalizing his experiences with her, the words she had spoken to him. She must still care. There was hope. If only he could get back, could see her, could talk to her . . . but that was ridiculous. He would stay here with the platoon until he was killed, or, by a piece of luck, wounded. He looked at the combat-packs whose owners never would wear them again, at the pierced helmets and the blood-stained gas-masks. Pieces of equipment were scattered over the ground alongside the small, pitiful holes which had been dug for safety. The tall, straight trees grew thicker in the distance. Their shadows invited him. The grass acted as a continual spring-board, pushing his body forward into the thicket. On he walked, a smile, half of gladness, half of bewilderment, turning up the corners of his mouth.

At last, out of sight of every one, in the thickest of the woods, he sat upon a small hill and regarded his misshapen, hobnailed shoe. It held a curious fascination for him. Yes, the little bump was where the small toe curled. But none of his other toes reached to the end of the shoe, he reflected. What nice leather. A shame to spoil such leather as this. Yes, a shame, and besides . . . from his pack he drew a small, round can of Argentina beef, which he balanced between his instep and the toe of his shoe. No harm in spoiling this! He wiggled his toes around in the shoe and felt squeamish. His hand felt for his pistol at his side. Yes, there it was and nicely oiled. He drew the pistol from the holster and aimed it at the small blue can. Forty-five-caliber pistols kicked up in the air when they were fired, he remembered. He aimed it a bit lower - and bang. For a moment he felt nothing. The grin was still on his face. Then his look changed to one of consternation. Better go back and report to the platoon. He rose to his feet, took a few steps, and fell to the ground. By heavens, this was no joke, shooting yourself in the foot. This was serious business. Hospital and everything. Then he remembered that he had done it himself. It was probably the first time that he had really known it. Court-martial and disgrace. And he had only meant to get back home. He began to whimper.

Lieutenant Harris, his skin the color of sun-bleached ash, walking among the men, was a beaten Napoleon. A patch of black, ragged beard, his heavy, bristling mustache, his dull brown eyes that seemed to pain, made him appear more dead than alive as he loped along. The men remained lying on the ground, recognizing his approach by a speculative glance. Their faces were interestingly similar. A dull gray pallor overspread them all. Their eyes were leaden, expressionless, save for a kind of apathetic fear of the inevitable. Each lower jaw hung at the same depressed angle. Lieutenant Harris sat down as if it were his final act.

"Any of you men feel like doing any work?" There was no answer. Lieutenant Harris spoke again. "I got to have a work detail. These fellows must be buried. Are there any volunteers?"

After a short silence someone asked weakly: "Where is that damned grave-digger battalion? What are they for?"

"Yes, where are they? I didn't come in this man's army to dig graves."

Lieutenant Harris tried to appear indignant. "How the hell do you expect the grave-diggers to be here when the artillery haven't even got up here yet? Nope, we've got to bury them, that's all. Besides, they're our dead. They'll be stinkin' like hell by tonight if we don't bury 'em," he encouraged. "Walker," he went on in a sort of drone, "pick out a burial detail and have the men work in reliefs." There was no "Yes, sir" forthcoming. The men looked at each other and then at Lieutenant Harris. "Walker ain't here."

"Did he get knocked off, too?" Lieutenant Harris asked.

"Naw, he was around here this morning."

"Does anybody know what happened to him? Where'd he go?"

No one knew.

"Well, if he's gone, he's gone." Lieutenant Harris grew decisive. "Rogers, you take charge. You don't need to bury 'em so deep. They'll have to be dug up again, anyway."

Rogers showed surprising signs of life. "All right, men." His accent became almost crisp. "Garrett, Morrow, Perry, Hartman, Edwards." He pointed his finger impressively as he named off five men.

Sullen, they rose and stood around hesitatingly, asking: "Where are the shovels? Do you expect us to dig holes with our hands?" Perry was weak and exasperated.

Rogers had become a dynamo and nearly purred with energy. "You'll find plenty of shovels right down by where Captain Anderson was killed. Follow me." The men trailed off in a group.

They set to work laboriously. Soon the first hole had reached a depth so that the bodies would not be too near the surface when the dirt was thrown back in place. On a bloody stretcher a mutilated body was carried to the freshly dug hole and rolled over upon a blanket.

"All right there, Morrow. Grab hold." Rogers was peremptory.

"Rogers, Ah can't. I'd throw up my guts. You call me when you're ready to dig the next hole." Morrow walked away.

"Come back here, Morrow. I'll report you for insubordination."

"Ah doan cah wot yo do. Go to hell."

While Rogers had been talking the body had been lifted into the hole and the first shovelful of dirt had been thrown over it.

"Say, wait a minute. Stop that. We've got to git his dog-tag off."

Rogers stooped over the body and fumbled at the dirty collar. "Gimme a knife." He snipped one of the identification disks from the greasy string. Stuffing it in his pocket, he drew back and ordered: "Now go ahead."

The business was continued silently. Bodies were carried to the clearing marked off for the temporary burial-place, rolled in a blanket, and dropped into shallow holes. Before they were dumped into their temporary graves their pockets were searched and the contents placed in little piles on the ground. Some of the bodies were unrecognizable, although the men at work had seen them and talked with them the day before. One or two of the bodies looked as if life had fled them peacefully. The uniforms were unspotted with blood, the faces were calm. But some of the faces were distorted. The lips rose from the teeth and made them look like fangs. One body, on which the skin was liverish, had been struck lifeless a few days earlier. It stunk terrifically, and when Rogers's hands sought out the neck for the identification tag, his fingers sank into the flesh. But he went stolidly on about his work. Garrett turned his body and engaged in a paroxysm of gagging. He turned again, his face the color of a piece of paper. The work went on.

The late afternoon sun shone upon a group of mounds of fresh-dug dirt. Each mound was marked by two rough sticks, made to form a cross, at the juncture of which a small aluminum disk bearing a number was fastened. A few yards away men were eating cold beef, cold boiled potatoes, and drinking lukewarm coffee from their muddy canteen cups.

The sky was clear and the air was like a bell. It could have been fancied that any noise must be a tinkling one. The tree tops were tall Gothic spires that reached to the heavens. The man in the moon was distinct in the round, pale ball that threw silvery sheets into the forest.

The platoon believed that it had embarked upon a night that at last was to be silent, harmless. They tried to stretch their muscles, which had been taut for days; their thoughts sought out other and more pleasant scenes of remembrance. The air was crisp and their bodies felt comfortable under their blankets. Their heads, pillowed on their gas-masks, were, for once, inert. Fear had flown.

The first shell that whined its course from the German lines to the place where they were asleep passed unnoticed. It struck the ground with a P-tt." The next one did likewise, but someone awakened. He touched the man lying near to him. "What was that?" he asked fearfully, wanting to be assured. Another shell, making a wobbly gurgling noise dropped several yards away.

"Oh, hell," said the aroused man. "The Squareheads are out of ammunition. They're shootin' beer-bottles over." He fell asleep, unconcerned. The first man sniffed. "Beer-bottles! I guess not. GAS!" he screamed, in a panic. Grunting, swearing, frightened, the men got their masks over their faces in less time than they had been trained to. Now they sat around tense, their minds blank, the saliva running down their chins from the mouthpiece of the mask.

Ahead of them, in the ravine, where they had been a few days ago, shells broke, reporting noisily. More shells were hurled over, to fall and explode, battering at the ravine. Meanwhile the barely discernible P-tt continued around them. The bombardment seemed to be everlasting. Under so heavy a bombardment the ravine must be leveled out. Bang, crash, bang, up in front at the ravine. P-tt, P-tt, P-tt, back where the platoon was lying. Out of the noise a voice was heard calling: "Hey, Third Platoon. We want volunteers for stretcher bearers!"

Through the dimness made by the glass eyes of his mask, Garrett saw a man come stumbling through the trees.

"Where are you, Third Platoon?" the form cried.

Garrett drew off his mask, yelled "HERE!" and replaced it, then forcing the contaminated air out of the mask.

"We want volunteers." The form had a querulous voice.

Garrett took off his mask again. "Put on your mask!" he shouted.

"Damn the mask!" cursed the form. "We've got nothing but wounded men up at the front line and we want some help."

From somewhere among the still figures Lieutenant Harris arose and walked to the form.

"Hello, Doc. You better put on your mask. The gas is damn heavy here." He dove into his mask again.

"Damn it, I came back here for volunteers, not to be told what to do. We got a lot of wounded men up there."

"All right; I'll get you some men." He summoned six men and ordered them to take litters up to the ravine.

CHAPTER SEVENTEEN

"Good God, Garrett, don't go so fast. Wait a minute."

"All right; let your end down, then."

Garrett and Peterson had been assigned to the job of litter bearers. It was now the third time that they had carried a wounded man from the ravine to the first-aid station, almost two miles away. To do so they had to escape the shells that fell so numerously in the ravine, and, with their masks on, to carry their burden through the gulley filled with gas. On arriving at the first-aid station the first time they found their burden to be dead. His arm had been severed from his body. The second man was unconscious when he was lowered to the ground in front of the first-aid station. Now they were on the way from the ravine once more, carrying a man whose middle had been pierced by a fragment of shell casing. As they lowered the stretcher to rest, the man groaned and pleaded with them to go on. Garrett tried to reason: "We'll never git there, if we don't take a little rest. We'll be there soon, buddy. Do you want a drink?" He offered his canteen.

"No, just take me away from here," the man groaned piteously.

They rested until they could endure the man's groaning no longer; then they started off. They had no more than started when a shell struck directly in rear of them. They plodded on with their burden, stumbling over the boulders in the gulley. A little farther on and another shell exploded. On they went until the mustard-like odor of gas filled their nostrils. Then they stopped to put on their masks.

Letting his end of the stretcher sink slowly to the ground, Garrett asked the wounded man: "Can you wear a mask, buddy?"

"Yes, oh, yes, give it to me. I'll die without it." Fear in the man's voice was stronger than pain.

Garrett bent over the man's chest for the familiar respirator. It was gone. "Where is your mask?" he asked.

"I don't know."

Gently Garrett raised the wounded man's head and placed his mask over the face of the wounded man. They started on again. Rapidly, successively, three shells struck close by. The rear end of the stretcher dropped to the ground.

"Peterson!" cried Garrett.

Peterson did not answer, and Garrett, putting down his end of the stretcher, walked to the other end and felt along the ground. Peterson was lying on his side. His neck was wet with blood. A large piece of shell casing had struck him below the ear, and he was now quite dead. His mask was in shreds.

The wounded man was unconscious.

Until he was hoarse and the gas had burned his eyes so that they were coals of fire, Garrett called for help. But none came. His eyes smarting dreadfully, Garrett wrapped his coat around his head and took up his night's vigil beside the wounded man. The bombardment continued most of the night.

When the sun made its pilgrimage over the rim of the distant field and showered the scene with light, Garrett was still sitting on a small rock beside the stretcher, his chin supported by his knees, the coat over his head.

For a distance of two miles, from the ravine to the village where the supply wagons were stationed, men lay dead and dying. In the woods and particularly in the gulley that ran through the woods to the village, the thick yellow gas clung to the ground. Whenever the gas had touched the skin of the men dark, flaming blisters appeared. Like acid, the yellow gas ate into the flesh and blinded the eyes. The ground was a dump-heap of bodies, limbs of trees, legs and arms independent of bodies, and pieces of equipment. Here was a combat pack forlorn, its bulge indicating such articles as a razor, an extra shirt, the last letter from home, a box of hard bread; another place a heavy shoe, with a wad of spiral puttee nearby. Where yesterday's crosses had been erected, a shell had churned a body out of its shallow grave, separating from the torso the limbs. The crosses themselves had been blown flat, as if by a terrific wind.

In the gray light of early morning Garrett felt the fury of impotence as he tried to rise. He unwound the coat that covered his head, forgetful, unmindful for the moment of the man whom he had guarded during the night. He seemed fastened to the surface of the stone. Dimly, he knew that his legs burned with an awful pain. But the feeling of pain was lost in his marveling at his inability to rise. Not far, distant voices sounded. Soon a detail of men filed along the gulley, commenting among themselves upon the havoc of the night. Garrett called weakly to the men who were approaching.

Garrett's mind was a blank, as if conscientiousness itself had a switch that could be maneuvered to the off position. Too much had occurred in such too little time for any person to comprehend. As unknown hands touched him he lost his senses and his next remembrance was concern with a badly jolting ambulance in which men all about him were groaning.

CHAPTER EIGHTEEN

It was the night for relief. Twelve men, with the remainder of their equipment about them, huddled around in a group waiting for the new troops to appear and take over their sector. They were tired, hungry, and nerve-racked; the word morale could not conceivably be associated with them. Their three weeks' experience in the woods had so bludgeoned their senses that they had been unresponsive even when told that they were to be relieved. But after a while they partly recovered under the stimulation of the picture of warm food and a shelter of comparative safety. From a thick apathy they became clamorous, ill at ease, waiting for the new men to come. As the darkness grew their nerves twitched, and they peered often and again down the gulley from which the relief was to come into sight. At last a muffled clatter reached their ears. It swelled and was accompanied by voices in a polyglot of tongues. Cigarette lights and the flare of matches were seen along the line of the incoming horde.

Lieutenant Harris had risen at their approach. Now he nervously shifted his weight from one leg to the other. "The drafted idiots," he muttered, "do they want to kill all of us with these lights? Hey, you guys," he called, "put out those damned matches." A swell of jeers greeted him.

"All right, Third Platoon, let's go. If these damned fools want every German gun to start pounding at them, let them. Come on!"

The platoon rose wearily and dragged through the woods in the direction of the village. Their spirits were so depressed, their bodies so fatigued, that, though the village was but two miles distant, an hour had elapsed before they marched through the cluttered streets between the rows of battered houses. But they did not stop. The outline of the village faded as they tramped. Behind them shells rumbled over from the German lines, and, in answer, the crack and the sudden flare of a large gun being fired sounded to the right and left of them. At the noise the men's muscles tightened, their nostrils narrowed and were bloodless. At the appearance of danger unheralded they were thorough automata; the explosions urged on their tired legs, whose muscles seemed tied in inextricable knots. Thick forests rose on each side of the tortuous white road, their dark tops bewitchingly patterned against the sky. Where the woods were divided by a narrow path the platoon turned off, marching between the trees.

Farther in the woods, where the path widened slightly, the men halted. In ten minutes they were curled up in their blankets, asleep.

The platoon awoke in the heat of the day. In the woods the leaves of the trees were unruffled by a breeze. Glaring down from directly above, the sun was a monstrous incinerator. But for it all nature would have been inanimate. The men stretched experimentally. Their empty intestines made them aware of themselves. From among the trees floated a rich odor of frying food. "Steak," someone guessed. The smell intensified their hunger, weakened them. Parker, shading the sun from his owl-like eyes, sat up and sniffed.

"Who said 'steak'?" he observed owlishly. "Smells like good old country fried chicken to me."

"Chicken, hell," said Hartman, the professional pessimist. "It's probably fried canned bill."[26]

---

[26] Canned beef.

"Oh, you make me sick," Parker answered. "Can't you let a man dream?"

But it was steak. And dipped in flour before it was fried. It was not choice steak, but it was edible, very edible. And the quantity had been prepared for sixty men, while there were only twelve men to dine.

"Go easy," cautioned Lieutenant Harris, gnawing a huge steak which he held in his hand. "There's plenty of chow, so you don't need to be in a hurry to eat it all. You'll do better if you eat slowly. Stomach's not used to this sort of food."

"Je's, this is jist like bein' home," Parker informed the assembly.

"Home? You never had a home. What are you talkin' about?" jeered Dempsey, the New York roughneck who had been confined in the hospital twice with delirium tremens. "Ho there, you yellow greaseball, what do you want?" He hailed one of the mess helpers who was approaching.

"I heard that Cornelius Dempsey got scairt and shot himself when he got up to the front, and I come down to see if it was true."

The greaseball, whose name described him well, looked inquiringly around. Dempsey failed to answer the badinage. The greaseball sat down among the men, who now had become filled and grew confidential. "You fellahs had a pretty tough time up there, didn't you?"

"I'll say we did."

"You'd a thought so if you'd a been there, you low-life."

"Yeh, pretty soft for you birds in the galley."

"But not as soft as it's goin' to be for you guys," the greaseball was ingratiating.

"Whaddya mean?" the platoon scoffed.

"Ain't you heard?" The greaseball looked surprised.

"Heard nothin'," Parker answered grumpily. "Where've we been to hear anything?"

"Well," hesitatingly, "maybe I hadn't ought to tell."

"Go on and tell, greaseball."

"Yeh, what the hell else are you good for?"

"Well . . . you guys ain't goin' back to the front no more."

"Hooray!" they skeptically shouted. "You damned liar."

"Fact. The Brigade Commander was down here yesterday, and I heard him tell Major Adams that the First Battalion was goin' on board ship."

"Oh-o. That ain't so good. I was sick all the way over on that damn transport," Morrow remembered aloud.

"Sure, you always do," said Hartman, the old-timer. "But after the first cruise you're all right. God, man, you don't know how soft it is on board ship. A clean bunk and good chow. Shore leave whenever you go into port. Why, I remember . . ."

"Maybe you're right, but I'll take my chances with my feet on the ground. There ain't no damn whale gonna eat me, not if I know it."

"Well, it's a blame sight better than lettin' them Squareheads use you for a target. I'm glad we're goin'."

While they talked the rumor that they had so skeptically regarded had become a fact. No one doubted that they were soon to be loaded into box cars and sent off to some seaport, where trim, clean ships would be waiting to take them abroad.

CHAPTER NINETEEN

Snorting gray camions drew up along the road by the path where the men were lying. At the driving-wheels the small Anamites with their long, tired mustaches covered with fine dust, looked like pieces of graveyard sculpture. The dust was over their faces, over their light-blue uniforms. They sat immovable. The men took their seats upon the narrow benches and the camions chugged away.

A river crawled along, its straight banks parallel with the road over which the camions were moving. In the crepuscular light it was a dark, straggly, insignificant stream, which, compared by the platoon with rivers that they had known, was only a creek. It was quite dark when the camions stopped at a town along the river, built in the valley between large hills. The men debarked and were assigned to their billets wherever empty rooms could be found in the houses.

In Nanteuil, the name of the village where they had stopped, the ranks of the platoon were filled by men from one of the replacement battalions that recently had arrived in France from the United States. A daily routine was quickly established, and with but one day's rest the platoon was kept at work from early morning until late afternoon. They drilled four hours a day, were inspected daily by the acting Company Commander, tried to rid themselves of lice by swimming in the Marne, made secret expeditions to neighboring villages, where they got drunk and made amorous eyes at sloppy French grandmothers, threw hand-grenades in the river and watched the dead fish rise to the surface, swore at the gendarmes[27] when those persons remonstrated with them, shrank into basements whenever the long-distance German shells were aimed at the bridge that crossed the river at Nanteuil, cursed their officers, and tried to scare the new men by exaggerating the frightfulness of the front, gorged themselves on the plentiful rations, and played black jack, poker, or rolled dice out of sight of their officers. The officers smiled and told each other that they were not only recovering their morale, but were imbuing the new men with that spirit peculiar to the Infantry.

The platoon had been in Nanteuil one week when Garrett returned, dusty, tired, and hungry. The older men crowded around him eagerly while the more recent members stood off wonderingly.

"Well, Garrett, old boy, did you have a good rest?" Morrow asked.

"Rest? Rest hell. The only way you can get a rest is to get killed. But don't go to the hospital thinking you'll get it." Garrett paused, sat down and lit a cigarette. "Remember that night they put over the gas attack?" He was assured by each of the old-timers that they did.

"Well, the next afternoon I woke up in an evacuation hospital. They carried me in on a stretcher, and when I opened my eyes there was a lousy doctor standing over me. 'What are you doing here?' he asked. Well, I could hardly talk, but I managed to whisper that I was gassed. He looked down at my card that the first-aid officer had pinned on me. 'God damn it, get up you coward,' he said to me. 'What the hell do you mean by taking a wounded man's place?' Of course, I was sore as hell, but what could I do? So I stuck around a while until an ambulance started for our battalion, and then I hid in it and came along."

The men cursed the medical officer effusively.

---

[27] A French police officer.

"Saw Walker back there," Garrett continued. "He was lyin' in bed with his foot in a sling. Said he got lost and some Squarehead shot him." Garrett threw the butt of his cigarette. "But if you think the medical officers are bad, you ought to see the enlisted men. Don't take any souvenirs back with you, if you go. The damn orderlies'll steal 'em. One guy had a Luger pistol and about four hundred francs when he got in the hospital, and they give him a bath, and when he comes out he hadn't a thing in his clothes. But I got a good hot bath, I'll say that much. And I got some clean clothes. The damned clothes I had stunk so of gas that they had to bury them."

"How was the chow?"

"Rotten. And you have to line up in the mud in your pajamas to get it, if you're a walking patient. They say the base hospitals are worse."

"Yeh, but you don't have no shavetail raggin' you around all the time, do you?"

"The hell you don't. Them damned orderlies who are supposed to do the work hand you a broom and tell you to clean up the deck, or wash up the latrines, or make up somebody's bed." Garrett got up and limped away. "Got to report to the Company Commander."

"How come you're limpin', Garrett?"

"Still got sores on my legs where that confounded gas burned."

The new men vowed that they never would be harmed.

After an hour's close order drill the next day Garrett was noticed to be unable to keep in step. Three times Lieutenant Harris bit his lip and refrained only by great repression from reprimanding him. When the platoon came to a halt, Lieutenant Harris moved over to Garrett and quietly and venomously asked: "Garrett, what the hell's the matter with you? Why the hell do you walk along like you had a brick in your pants?"

"I'm sorry, but I can't help it, Lieutenant Harris. I still have sores on my legs."

"Well, what are you doing back here then? Fall out and report to the first-aid station at once." Lieutenant Harris was exasperated.

Garrett limped out of sight. But after that he did not drill with the platoon. Each day when they set out he watched them from the window of the bare room where his squad was billeted. And each day the sergeant of the Medical Corps secretly treated him for his burns. At the close of a week Garrett was well, and when orders were received for the platoon to move he was quite ready.

Then began a dismal time; when, almost invariably, the platoon had been marched into some woods at night and had made their beds on the ground, they would be ordered to make up their equipment and be ready to march in an hour or less. Thus, they lived in the woods in the daytime and at night marched from one forest to another.

Not even the officers could give a reason for the senseless maneuvering. It was during this time that the rumor became common that they were to board battleships and effect a landing party on the Mole; they also were to be sent to southern France to a rest camp as soon as their barracks near Marseilles had been completed; they also were to be returned to the United States and be split up to serve as recruiting officers and instructors to the drafted men. These rumors, and the occasional rations of cigarettes they were given, helped them to endure their nightly pilgrimages and their cramped daily lives in the woods.

And then one day, when they had despaired ever of doing anything but moving through the night from one clump of woods to another, an order was received for the platoon to be ready to entrain on camions at three that afternoon. They did not know whether to rejoice or not.

The march was more weary than even they had expected. They had left the camions early that morning and had begun a climb up a long, punishing hill whose summit seemed in the clouds. On this road the marching was even, steady. There was no body of troops in front of the platoon to cause it to halt, stand with heavy packs cutting through the shoulder muscles, and then march on again. A forest on one side, the scene stretched out on the other a long, flat prairie of glistening wheat. On and on they marched, reaching the summit of the hill and escaping the sun where large, tall trees bowed in a canopy over the road. Noon came and day disappeared; the shadows threw themselves fantastically upon the road, and still the platoon continued its steady tramp. The air grew cool. It found an easy entrance through the slight clothing of the men and covered their bodies with a dampness. Darkness found them heavily pounding out the miles along the road. Men began grumbling, threatening to fall out along the roadside. They were indignant at not having rested, at not being fed. One man, desiring to drink, reached for his canteen and found it empty. His voice rose plaintively in the stillness. Other men felt thirst. They made known their desires in language reproachful and uncomplimentary to their officers.

At midnight the platoon stopped. It turned into the woods and lay down. Orders were passed among the men to dig holes in the ground for protection. "We'll be here all night," the officers said, "and there may be an attack before we shove off."

The men greeted the order by failing to move. Several of them muttered that they didn't give a damn whether the enemy attacked or not. Suddenly, out of the thick blackness of the woods and the night a six-inch gun barked and recoiled, barked again and recoiled. The shells sped through the night, striking, aeons afterward, with the noise of a pricked balloon. Another salvo shot over into the darkness, the ignition of the charge lighting up a small distance of woods and throwing the trees into crazy relief. Three shells, large ones, raced each other over the enemy lines. They struck with a clatter, as if they had felled half of the forest. All along the line long-range rifles fired their huge bolts of explosives toward the enemy. Small seventy-fives barked like little dogs running after an automobile. In retaliation the shrill shriek of the German shells answered. On both sides the batteries continued pounding away. An orderly, parting the brush and making a noise like a stampede of wild horses, appeared and asked to be directed to the Company Commander. Five minutes afterward the platoon was given orders to move forward. To the tune of heavy artillery battering away like enormous drums the platoon, joined at each end by other units of the division, felt its way blindly through the forest. When the sun rose they were still working their way through the trees. Unexpectedly, the guns in the rear of the moving lines stopped. The battle of Soissons had begun.

CHAPTER TWENTY

The platoon was first apprised of the nearness of the enemy when Parker raised his rifle and fired quickly. He had seen a soiled gray uniform skirting among the trees a few yards ahead. A quick electric shock ran from shoulder to shoulder along the advancing line. The platoon stopped for a moment as if stunned. Then they advanced without increasing their pace. In their faces a machine-gun spat angrily, the bullets flying past like peevish wasps. Automatic rifles were manipulated in the middle of the automatic rifle squad, and the loaders took their places at the sides of the men who were firing, jamming in one clip of cartridges after another. Rifle bullets fled past the advancing men with an infuriating zing. The Maxim machine-guns kept up a rolling rat-t-t-tat cold objective.

The platoon had reached the first machine-gun nest, almost without knowing it. There were three Germans, their heavy helmets sunk over their heads, each performing a definite part in the firing. They, too, were surprised. Morrow, a little in the lead, drew a hand-grenade from his pocket, pulled out the pin, and threw it in their faces. It burst loudly and distinctly. One German fell flat, another grasped at his arm, his face taking on a blank expression as he did so, while the last man threw his hands above his head. Inattentive to his gesture of surrender, the line pushed on.

The fighting grew more furious. Germans, surprised, were hiding behind trees and firing their slow-working rifles. When the advancing line would reach them they would receive a charge of shot in their bodies, sometimes before they had fired at the swiftly moving line.

Some member of the platoon offered his version of an Indian war whoop. It was successful in hastening the attack. Exhilarated, but sheerly impotent, one man ran forward blubbering, "You Goddamn Germans," and pointing an empty rifle at the trees. Other men calmly and methodically worked the bolts of their rifles back and forth, refilling the chambers as they were emptied of each clip of five shots. From time to time a man dropped, thinning the ranks and spreading them out to such an extent that contact on the right side of the moving line was lost.

Farther on in the woods a small trench had been dug, but through the fierceness and unexpectedness of the attack most of the enemy had been driven from it. The platoon, moving on feet that felt like wings, dashed toward the trench, some of the men sprawling into it. Before them, a few yards distant, a machine-gun poked its nose from between the crevice of two large rocks. The sight of it infuriated Lieutenant Harris, who was leading the platoon by a few paces. Then, yards away, he began throwing bombs at it. His last bomb exhausted, he aimed his pistol and chucked the remaining shots at it. Now, almost able to look over the top of the rock and see the gunner, he threw the useless pistol at the heavy steel helmet. The gunner dropped his head, covering it with his hands. When he looked up, the platoon had passed. Farther, the resistance grew less. The bombardment of the night before had taken its toll of Germans. Bodies lay gawkily about on the grass. One body, headless, clutched a clay pipe between its fingers. Another lay flat on its back, a hole in its stomach as big as a hat. A heavy leather pack, which a shell had struck, was the center of a ring of packages of Piedmont cigarettes which its owner had salvaged from some dead American.

The trees became sparse. Ahead, over an interminably long wheatfield, the platoon could see the horizon. There were no Germans in sight. The platoon, ordered to do so, faced in the direction from which they had come and combed the woods for machine-gun nests which they might have passed unnoticed during the attack.

In their poignant hunger the men forgot even to look for pieces of German equipment which they might sell to Y.M.C.A. men and others of the personnel behind the lines. But each leather German pack was searched for food, and canteens were picked up, shaken, and either thrown down with disgust or hastily put to the men's lips and greedily drained of whatever might be in them. There were loaves of black bread which, in spite of the moldy look that was common to them all, were devoured; an occasional comb-of-honey was found. Morrow, exploring one of the packs, drew forth a pair of baby stockings and a small knitted hood. Beside the pack lay a peaceful-looking, home-loving German who had passed his middle years.

"Here's an orphan, all right!" Morrow announced, and went to the next pack.

They were nearing a clump of bushes when a young German stepped out. His face was the color of putty and his eyes brought to Garrett the picture of an escaped convict hunted by bloodhounds in a Southern swamp. His hands were high above his head, as high as their frightened nerves would permit them to be. At the sight of him an uncouth, illiterate tatterdemalion[28] from the south of Illinois snarled half animal-like, raised his rifle to his shoulder and fired directly at the prisoner. A look of surprise, utter unbelief, came over the man's face as he dropped heavily to the ground. "Damn ye, that'll larn ye ta stay hum." The fellow, his thin evil face grimaced with hatred, walked over and spat expertly a stream of tobacco juice at the already dead body. Garrett looked on nonplussed, not knowing whether his companion had done the ethical thing or not. Was this what war was all about: becoming the enemy to conquer the enemy?

---

[28] Raggedly dressed and unkempt.

Hot and tired, knowing nearly every need of the body, Garrett neared the place where he had entered the woods late the night before, as the sun was sinking out of sight.

He arrived at a crossroads and turned to the right. Thick woods, green at the fringe and black within, walled the smooth white gravel road on either side. Through soft, fluffy clouds that floated over an inanely-blue sky, the sun volleyed rays of brilliant light. Small, shiny pebbles, reflecting the glint, were transformed into pretty baubles of crystal and amber.

On the right of the road, moving forward in an unbroken stream, plodded a single file of drab-colored men. From a distance the line looked like a swaying, muddy snake. In the middle of the road, also moving forward, black, roan, and sorrel horses pulled caissons, field kitchens, and supply wagons. Men returning from the direction, in which the main traffic was moving, were on the left. They passed by, dejected, vapid-minded, a look of dull pain in the eyes of each. They were the wounded from the attack. Most spectacular among them were the French Colonials, with their red kepis, their broad chests showing strength and endurance beneath their blue or tan tunics. Occasionally a mass of white, blood-stained gauze would be wrapped around a black, shiny head, and strong white teeth would be doggedly bared with pain. The small carbines and long knives that they carried set them off as a special sort of troops. And then the French, with their horizon-blue uniforms and drooping, inevitable mustaches, shoulders sagging, slouched along with bandaged heads and bandaged arms. And the gray of the German uniform and the thump, thump of the leather boots that they wore. Small, hideous caps, round and gray, with a thin red piping circling the top, set awkwardly on their heads, which rose from thick fat necks. Behind them walked surly, wary Frenchmen with long-rifles. A number of English troops were scattered through the unending line. Beside the Americans whom they passed their khaki uniforms looked smart and tailored. In this multicolored canyon no words were exchanged. The Colonials looked sullen, the French beaten and spiritless, the Americans dogged and conscientious, the English expressionless; the Germans seemed the most human of them all. For them the fighting was finished.

Miles from the place where the platoon had alighted from the camions another road split the deep wall of green forest, and at the crossing a large farmhouse stood in the middle of a large field. Whitewashed, all but the roof, it looked like a cheap but commodious burial vault, with the yard in the rear filled high with dead and wounded. The first place of shelter from the actual front, it was being used as a dressing station for the maimed. Many of the men brought back wounded had died here; in a pile made like carelessly thrown sticks of wood their bodies now lay. There those whom an imaginary line had named friend and enemy shared a common lot. German bodies and Austrian mingling and touching French, Belgian; their positions a gruesome offering to the God of War. All day long the heavy hobnailed boots of hurriedly advancing men had beaten out a requiem.

The platoon filed along to the left upon the crossroad, marching as swiftly as their tired legs would permit. The stream of wounded had stopped. The field kitchens and supply wagons had turned off in the woods in the rear. For miles sounded the baffled roar of firing artillery. Now and then a man fell out alongside the road, unable to march any longer, the cool green of the grass in the late afternoon offering a tantalizing bed. From behind them commenced a great clatter of caissons drawn jerkily along the shell-torn road by galloping, lathered horses. Artillerymen, one on the back of the leading horse, two on the caisson seat, urged the horses forward with picturesque curse words, only stopping long enough to shout at the platoon: "Better hurry up, you guys, or we'll git to Germany before you will." They rumbled away.

In a twilight of mauve the platoon came to a halt on the crest of a broad hill. Silently they deployed, mud-caked ghosts, dragging wearily and uncertainly out in a long line that offered its front to the challenging boom of the enemy's long-range guns. Water was found in a spring nearby, and the men lay down in the shallow holes that they had dug, their blankets and ponchos thrown over them. A solitary sentry watched the stars, watched the red, the green, the blue-and-white signal lights flare for a moment along the line, then die away.

The gray spirit of dawn rose and hovered over the ground. In the faint light a unit of cavalry filed past. The riders, on delicate, supple mounts, carried long lances, with their points skyward. On their blue helmets bright, feathery plumes fell back gracefully. Their spotless uniforms, gray in the morning light, set off their youthful figures like those of pages attending a mediaeval court. The horses, their fine legs delicately contoured, minced daintily down the hill and out of sight.

Ahead, through a scattered line of trees, stretched a spacious prairie, covered thick with wheat, a slightly rolling sea, majestically and omnipotently engulfing the universe.

The platoon rose stiffly, bewildered, rubbing the stiffness from their faces. Over the calm of the air a danger was born. Men smelled it in the acrid odor of powder which covered the grass. The trees, a thin line before them, swayed poignantly. Lorelei,[29] singing seductively, sat in their branches. In attack formation the platoon moved toward the trees, to the front toward which they were advancing.

On the farther side of the fringe of trees and running parallel with them was a path. Reaching it, the platoon turned to the left, tramping heavily toward the main road from which they had come the night before.

Scuffing the dust with lagging feet, the men crawled along the dusty road, lined on each side by contorted faces of soldiers who had come to support the line of attack. Farther down the road a small town lay half hidden in the valley. Long, slender smoke-stacks rose amid a

---

[29] Lorelei was an Asgardian sorceress who could use her voice to ensnare the minds of men.

cluttering of small deserted houses, where, twenty-four hours earlier, German soldiers had been quartered. Through one of the chimneys of the factory a three-inch shell had ploughed its way, stopping with the nose protruding from one side, the butt from the other. There it was suspended, implicit in its obedience. Interminably long words were printed on signs over the doors of the houses. At a street crossing the old names of the thoroughfares had been blotted out, and such names as Kaiserstrasse and Wilhelmstrasse were roughly lettered over them. There was a touch of impiety, of great barbarousness, in the changing of names which for so long had been honored. Also a very strong suggestion of a sound, thorough business administration having been instituted in place of the lax, pleasant manner of the village before the war. A peculiar, disagreeable odor hinted at great and ruthless thrift. The Germans had been careful of their dead. None remained lying on the street.

The platoon wound through the town and out upon the wheat-field which that morning they had viewed through the scraggly trees. Dazzling sunlight beat upon the full-topped yellow heads of wheat that weighted down the cool green stalks; on the flat, absurdly shaped helmets of the soldiers; on the sharp white bayonets raised above the wheat with which the field was filled. Deploying, the men halted, joined on either side by other men with silly-looking helmets, rifles, and bayonets.

From the road a small tank labored up the hill, puffing and creaking in every joint. Another tank, a miniature of the tanks pictured in the recruiting posters, wheezed along on its caterpillar tread. More tanks came. They were all small, ineffectual-looking little monsters, wearing a look of stubborn, gigantic babies. The arrival of the tanks was greeted by the firing of a salvo of shells from the German lines.

The platoon lay down in the wheat, trying to shield their bodies from the sight of the enemy. But the tanks, wheeling and rearing and grinding like devils gnashing their teeth, made perfect targets for the long-range shells. With their small, ridiculous gun-barrels pointing in three directions through holes in their steel armor, they were delightfully impervious to the havoc they were causing the Infantry. And their silly camouflage, into the making of which some painter had put his soul - reds and greens, the colors of autumn leaves, black and modest browns - in all their disguise they were as apparent at a distance of one thousand yards as large white canvases with black bull's-eyes and rings scored on them. For an everlasting half-hour they ploughed and squirmed through the field, struggling to get into position in order that the attack might commence. Meanwhile shells, timed like the ticking of a clock, fell with horrible and spirit-shaking accuracy. At last the tanks had maneuvered themselves into the proper distance ahead of the front line. Whistles were blown piercingly. The advance, the men aligned in four waves, had commenced.

Garrett, lying in the wheat-field, divided his attention between the maneuvering of the tanks and the frantic scampering of the insects on the ground and in the wheat, whose manner of existence he had disturbed when he sat down. Black little creatures, they waddled over the ground with as great a seriousness and importance as if they supported the burden of the world. Disorganized, they ran in all directions, even toward Garrett's hobnailed boots and upon his awkwardly rolled puttees. It was the first time since he had enlisted that he had thought much about bugs, save for the kind that infest the body. Now he wondered whether their lives were not as important as the lives of men; whether they were not conscious of a feeling that, were they no longer to exist, the end of the world would come. He compared them with the hustling, inane little tanks, and almost concluded that one was as important as the other. He stood by carefully so as not to step on any of the insects.

So far the German shells had burst either far behind the platoon or far in front. But now the whine, ever increasing, of a shell informed him that in a moment he would be listening to the ripping sound of flying pieces of shell casing. He waited, breathless. Fifteen yards behind him the shell exploded terrifically. He looked back. "Oh, Larkson," he called. Larkson was nowhere to be seen. "Damn these tanks," he fretted. "They'll have us all killed, first thing we know."

The dread of the attack was forgotten in the more immediate danger of the enemy artillery finding the exact range of the platoon by means of the sputtering tanks. A flock of shells left the long, black mouths of the German guns and began their journey toward Garrett. He winced, tied his muscles into knots, and threw himself flat on the ground, quite forgetful of the insects. The shells all struck within a radius of twenty yards, throwing up dirt, grain, a black cloud of smoke. The whistle blew and Garrett rose again.

As he started forward, abreast of the first wave, he had never before felt so great a stiffness in his legs, nor so great a weight in his shoes. It was as if they were tied to the earth. For a moment the jargon and melody of a once-popular song flooded his brain. Then he thought of the platoon joke about the man from the wilds who had come barefoot to a Recruiting Officer to enlist, and who, upon putting on a pair of shoes, had stood still for hours, believing that he was tied to the floor. "Ha," thought Garrett, "that's a funny one. They had to put sand in his shoes before he would move."

War was a business of tightening things, he observed, as he fastened the chin strap of his helmet more tightly. Corroborating the evidence, he drew in his belt over his empty stomach. The men were marching along, an interval of three yards between each. A shell struck directly upon the moving front wave a few yards to the left of Garrett. An arm and a haversack foolishly rose in the air above the cloud of smoke of the exploding shell. Slightly farther on machine-guns began an annoying rat-tat-tat, the bullets snipping off the heads of grain. More men fell. The front rank went on with huge gaps. On they stolidly marched. Garrett, glancing back, saw that the four waves had been consolidated into but two. But the bayonets glistened as brightly as before.

"Close in there, Garrett," somebody yelled, and Garrett asked whether the men were not being killed swiftly enough, without grouping them together more closely. They advanced to a point where they were enfiladed by the enemy's machine-guns. As the four lines had become two, so now the two lines became one. But on they marched, preserving a line that could have passed the reviewing stand on dress parade.

Beyond a cluster of trees was a village which had been named as the objective of the attack for that day. The road, canopied by green tree boughs, led to it from the town which that morning the platoon had left. The road was level, more level even than the field. It made a path as directing as a bowling-alley for the machine-gunners and riflemen in the village. Thus, the road was almost a certain death-trap for anyone who tried to cross. The right section of the platoon had begun the attack on one side of the road, the left on the other. As the ranks thinned and a greater distance between each man was required to preserve contact with the advancing line, the men on the right, where the heavier firing occurred, spread out, drawing away from the road.

The shells continued to fall, using as their target the slowly moving tanks which regulated the advance of the Infantry. Suddenly a large six-inch shell struck the turret of the tank nearest the platoon. The tank recoiled and stood stock-still. A moment later two men, like frightened rabbits, scurried out of the tank and ran back toward the rear.

Three airplanes, white stars in a field of red on their wings, flew gaily over the field and toward the German lines. They floated gracefully and haughtily out of sight. Not much later on they precipitately returned with three Fokkers[30] after them like angry hornets. Shriven of their grandeur, they flocked in disorder back to their hangars, the machine-guns of the German planes spitting bullets after them. The aerial entertainment was changed: four large German bombing planes, pursuing a businesslike course, arrived above the advancing men and began to drop bombs and fire machine-gun bullets at them. The bombs reported as noisily as the seventy-seven millimeter guns, but they made only a shallow hole in the ground. More devastating were the machine-gun bullets which zinged off the steel helmets of the men or bored their way through to the skull. Under the combination of direct artillery fire, enfilade machine-gun, rifle sniping, bombs dropped from airplanes, the ranks of the advancing men had become so sparse that the attack was brought to a temporary halt.

---

[30] German airplanes.

CHAPTER TWENTY-ONE

It was now afternoon and the heat of the sun was unendurable. It burned upon the helmets and through the clothing and caused sweat to trickle down the skin, irritating the scratches, bruises, and burns with which the bodies of the men were covered. The four bombing planes continued lazily to circle overhead, kicking out their tail-gates,[31] as the men graphically phrased it. Garrett and Morrow, with four of the new men, were at the farthest point of advance. Lying flat, they tried with their bayonets, their mess knives, to throw up a protection of ground in front of them. Thoroughly tired, they worked slowly, in spite of the danger. They were halfway finished when a bullet zipped through the wheat and penetrated the bone of the crooked elbow with which the man next to Garrett was supporting himself.

"Here it is," said Garrett, picking up a small steel-jacketed bullet.

"By God, that hurts, cried Howell. "Help me get my shirt off."

"Je's, you're lucky," Garrett murmured enviously. "You'll never come back to the front any more. And what a fancy place to get hit!" The shirt off, the bullet was seen to have gone through the forearm just above the elbow, coming out on the other side.

"Don't you think so?" eagerly. "It don't hurt so much."

---

[31] Dropping bombs.

"No, but you better hurry up and git outa here or you'll have somep'n more than a busted arm," one of the new men advised.

The arrival of a salvo of shells decided the new man upon an immediate departure. Throwing away all of his equipment, he hurried away, his elbow pressed closely to his side.

Behind Garrett, a few yards, someone began to whimper.

"What's the trouble, buddy?"

"I d-d-on't kn-now," the voice stuttered, half sobbing, half crying.

"Well, why don't you beat it back?"

"I'm af-f-fraid."

"Damn it, get the hell out of here. Do you want us to go nutty with your bawlin'!" This from one of the new men.

"You've got a good excuse to go back, you know," Garrett assured. "Go back with Howell. A wounded man's supposed to have somebody go back with him."

"I c-c-can't-t. I went b-back once s-s-shell-shocked, and the d-doctors raised hell with me. I'm af-f-frai-d-d to go back again." The man started to laugh unpleasantly. His laughter changed to violent sobbing.

The men grew doubly frightened. "I can't stay here and hear that," one of them said. "It takes all the starch out of me." But he didn't move.

Near the road Parker lay upon the ground, his lips pressed against the dirt. By his head his hands were clinched, the knuckles flat. His helmet had fallen forward so that it covered his brow, but not the back of his head. His legs were as rigid as death. On his right leg the puttee had become unwound, the spiral-shaped cloth stringing out behind. The leather worn through by much marching, a glimpse of his bare foot appeared where the sole of his shoe had worn through. His shirt was tattered, and in the middle of his back a large hole had been blown. Surprisingly, there was very little blood on his shirt or upon any other part of his body save where the gaping hole showed the raw flesh. Hours earlier Parker had been struck by the explosion of a shell. Since then he had lain - alive.

A molten mass of flaming gold all day, the sun, from sheer exhaustion of vengeful burning, dropped weakly out of sight. Declining, it filled the sky with mauve and purple, gold and crimson designs. Swaying mournfully in the wisps of evening wind, the full heads of grain were like slender lances raised by an army of a million men. The village ahead, toward which the platoon had advanced within a distance of five hundred yards, was a vague blur against the soft gray sky.

It was an hour before nightfall, and firing along the front had partly ceased. The men in the advance line were lying prone, thankful for the surcease offered by the approaching night. Heard behind them was a swishing sound. Garrett turned, forgot even for the moment the piteous moans of the shell-shocked man when he saw troops swiftly walking.

"We're going to be relieved. We're going to be relieved." The thought pounded through his brain. The oncoming troops were now near and distinct. Garrett could see the red, brimless stovepipe hats, the black, shiny faces, the picturesque and decorated tunics of the Senegalese. They carried small rifles and long knives and looked frightfully dangerous. Garrett reflected that these were the fellows who were supposed to treasure the ears of the enemy as keepsakes. Swiftly, their huge leg muscles bulging under their puttees, they walked through the wheat and passed. Garrett felt dismal.

"Relief, hell. They're going to attack."

And they were. As silent as ghosts they fled straight for the village. The enemy, seeing them, opened up with their rifles and machine-guns with extraordinary furiousness. The black soldiers advanced unhesitatingly. Some of them dropped flat, never to rise again of their own volition, others clasped a hand to the part of the body where a bullet had entered and turned back, walking quickly and nervously, but failing to speak. Garrett had never seen so many men wounded without their exclaiming. Usually, when some American was struck he would cry some such absurdly obvious statement as "Oh, my God, I'm hit." A German would shriek his inevitable "Kamerad." A Frenchman would jabber. But these fellows - Garrett marveled. But the remaining five hundred yards were too difficult to cross. Where five of the fleet blacks set valiantly forth, but one of them returned.

Darkness fell, closing the world in on four sides. Off to the left, on the farther side of the road, a tank suddenly and unexpectedly burst forth with an internal explosion. Its grim little body showed solidly in the glorious blazing red. The report that followed sounded as if the armor of the tank would have been burst into a million pieces. Up shot another flare of redness, brightening the sky. As if there were some understanding among them, two other tanks began, at regular intervals, to belch their fireworks into the air. It was a wondrous sight. Far enough away not to be harmful, it had also the advantage of being a spectacle uninspired by malice or hatred. It was a thing in itself, a war of its own, in which no one shared, totally objective, non-utilitarian and spontaneous. Garrett gleefully considered the sight. But after a while the sideshow stopped and the dampness stole through the clothing of the men. A lone star twinkled forth, trembled violently for a moment and then disappeared. In the heat of the day many of the platoon had thrown away their blankets. Now they lay shivering with cold and fear and hopelessness.

Over the wheat-field the night mist hung like a thick, wet, flapping blanket. Elephantine, it touched against the faces of the men, sending shivers along their spines. Machine-gun bullets spattered perfunctorily. The shell-shocked man moaned like a banshee. Disgusted, feeling as if his stomach were about to crawl away from his body, Garrett rose, deciding to cross the road and find out whether there was any possibility of relief before dawn.

On the other side of the road the ground was softer and the men had dug deeper holes. The little mounds of freshly thrown dirt were hardly perceptible.

"Where's Lieutenant Harris?" Garrett asked in a low voice.

"Dead as hell," he was answered.

"Then who's in charge?"

"I am."

"Who's that, Thomas?"

"Yeh."

"When are we going to be relieved?"

"We're standing by now. They ought to be here any minute."

"Well, if that's so, I'm gonna take my squad back. We're pretty bad off, way up there, and one of the new fellows is making such a hell of a lot of noise that I'm afraid the Squareheads will begin firing again."

"'S'matter with him?"

"Shell-shocked, I guess."

"Well, maybe you'd better shove off."

Garrett felt his way back through the darkness, through the curtain of mist.

Supporting the weaker man between them, the small party moved off, with Garrett in the lead. He was travelling lightly, with little equipment. At the first of the advance he had thrown away his pack, containing an empty condiment can and three boxes of hard bread. Finally, he had disposed of all but his pistol, belt, canteen, helmet, and respirator. Leaving, he threw away his automatic rifle and the musette bag in which ammunition was supposed to be carried. He walked along, his chin high, stepping briskly through the hip-high wheat. Somewhere beyond was rest and security, warm food, and plenty of blankets.

It irked him that the rest of the squad did not walk as swiftly as he walked. His ears seemed to flatten against his head at being held back. The distance was so alluring. It promised so many things of which his body was in want. There was the hot coffee. Garrett fancied that he could smell the soul-satisfying aroma. He remembered that the American army little knew the value of coffee to the man who is cold and tired and awake in the early dawn. But there would be, no doubt, French galleys, with black kettles in which they brewed strong black chicory. Hot coffee! He thought of it and felt ready to faint. At any moment a shell might drive into the ground near him and blow him high in the air. Reins seemed fastened to his shoulders, holding them back, delaying his progress. He wanted to cry out against the inhumanity of being forced to walk so slowly in so dangerous a place after the work in hand was done. He thought of forging ahead, of leaving the blubbering man to himself. He measured the distance back to the woods and guessed the length of time it would take to arrive. An hour at the most. But if he ran he could make it in half an hour. The responsibility of the safety of the squad held him back. Revolted at his cowardly thoughts, he offered to help carry the burden.

The men objected. "You lead the way."

But Garrett was insistent. With one arm of the blubbering, nerveless mass around his neck, he forged ahead, feeling powerful and exultant under the added weight.

Whining lazily over their heads, gas shells soared and struck softly in the town in front of them. They reached the valley and passed down into the town. Over the ground and on the weeds a coating of yellow had formed. The air was heavy with an asphyxiating smell. The yellow from the ground bit through the puttees and penetrated the clothing; the odor was inhaled in deep gulps that caused the men to choke.

There was a moment of indecision in which the men hesitated between putting on their respirators, thereby retarding their steps, or hurrying through the town, their lungs exposed to the poisonous gas. With the shells continuing to come over in droves, it was not difficult to decide. The men breathed in the gas.

Had they not, they would not have seen the aperture in the side of the gulley, where a gas blanket covered a dugout filled with wounded. There they stopped, while Garrett informed the receiving officer that their burden had been badly gassed. He said nothing about his being shell-shocked.

Relieved of the great impedimenta, their progress quickened, and they were through the town almost as soon as they could have wished.

CHAPTER TWENTY-TWO

Before daybreak they arrived at the woods where the Battalion had been ordered to assemble. On entering the woods, Garrett was halted by one of the company Lieutenants who had offered to remain out of the attack in order that, should the Company be annihilated, he would be able to form the nucleus of another Company with the orderlies of the officers, the soiled assistants of the kitchen, and the like. Garrett, having thrown away most of his equipment, had annexed on the road to the woods parts of uniforms of all descriptions. On his head was a bright red kepi which formerly had belonged to a French Colonial. A pair of soft leather boots that reached above the calves of his legs had been salvaged from some officer's bedding roll. His blouse had been discarded and his shirt was unbuttoned at the throat. Hanging in cowboy fashion, a forty-five caliber Colt flapped against his right hip. From his left side was a Luger pistol that he had taken from a dead German officer.

Thus, he was a sight that no strictly military officer who had received at least ninety days' training in learning the commands of squads right, port and present arms, at some officers' training school could bear.

"Corporal!" the officer shouted indignantly. "What are you doing out of uniform?"

"I don't know, sir."

Truthfully, Garrett did not know. He only knew that he had thrown away much of his own equipment and that he was highly pleased with the equipment he had substituted.

"Don't know?" The officer was scandalized. "Corporal, how long have you been in the service?"

"Since war was declared," Garrett answered promptly.

"And you don't yet know how to dress? Nor how to address an officer? Corporal, you have not saluted me!" The officer was horror-stricken; his tone suggested an utter unbelief in Garrett's existence.

"You don't salute officers at the front, sir."

The officer turned green. "Corporal, consider yourself under arrest."

"Yes, sir." Garrett started to walk away.

"And Corporal," the officer called. "If you aren't back in uniform by the next time I see you, a charge of disobedience will be added to your offense."

"Yes, sir," Garrett muttered, walking away.

He sought out the coolest-looking spot in the woods and there lay down. In a moment he was asleep. In another moment he was awakened by a terrific noise. Unwittingly, he had selected for his bed a space not ten yards from where a battery of long-range guns were concealed. When they were fired the earth shook. He rose and fled farther into the woods.

Ahead of him, at the side of a green knoll, several old Frenchmen were pottering around a field kitchen. The coals of the wood fire under a huge black kettle glowed in a warming friendly fashion. The aroma of black, satisfying coffee steamed from the wide mouth of the caldron. Garrett was enchanted, powerless to move, afraid to approach the benignant genii. He felt like a vagrant, nose pressed against the window of a fashionable restaurant. But no, not like a vagrant. Vagrants were only in cities, in blessed civilizations. He was still undecided, when one of the squat little figures, that somehow reminded him of the characters in *Rip Van Winkle*, looked up. To Garrett he spoke unintelligibly, but his voice was not forbidding. Garrett came nearer. He sniffed. "Cafe?" he questioned.

"Oui, cafe," the man grunted, going on about his business.

"Cafe bon," offered Garrett.

"Oui. Cafe bon, tres bon," the man conceded.

"J'ai faim."

"O pardon. Vous avez faim. Voulez-vous cafe?" He scooped a ladleful of hot coffee from the caldron and offered it to Garrett. How simple it was, Garrett thought, as he drained the dipper.

The men gathered around Garrett. "Americain, oui?" They apparently had decided before offering the question. "Pas Anglais? Anglais mauvais."

They learned that he had been in the attack. "Boche pas bon aussi, non?"

From their bags cakes of chocolate and slices of bread were brought and offered. Garrett ate shyly but greedily.

They were the first Frenchmen whom he had tried to talk with since the day of the first attack of his platoon. Then they were disheartened, not caring whether the Germans drank beer from the Arc de Triumph or not. Now, they had regained heart and were willing to continue the struggle of the advance toward Germany. Garrett learned that he had engaged in the initial attack of a vast offensive, that the goal had been reached, that Soissons had fallen under the storm of the First and Second Regular Divisions, that Chateau-Thierry had at last been cleared of the enemy by the Third and Twenty-sixth Divisions, that in between the Fourth Regular Division had been successful in its attack.

"Fini la guerre?" asked Garrett, and he was frowned upon by the genii. No, they informed him, the war had begun anew and would continue long. The genii spoke of the black forest, of the Kriemhilde Stellung, which had never been passed save by Allied prisoners, of the narrowing front the German retreat would make. No, the war would last one year, two years, three years.

Garrett tramped through the forest, stumbling over large holes that had been torn in the ground by the explosions of German long-range shells. Now, all was quiet. The green leaves of the trees fluttered unperturbed, birds trilled from joy or shrieked messages to one another. The boughs of the trees were kind, shielding the men from the rays of the hot summer sun. Soldiers were bustling about, tugging ant-like at heavy caissons which seemed unwilling to budge.

Thoroughly tired out, men were stretched upon the cool grass asleep, forgetful of the void in their stomachs. Suddenly, in the distance, a very erect form stalked through the trees. As it approached, a thin, haughty face, above which a steel helmet jauntily set, was to be seen. At the sight of him all of the sleeping men arose as if by a signal earlier agreed upon. The tired, worn-out, hungry soldiers; the dirty, blood-smeared, lousy soldiers; the red-eyed, gas-eaten, mud-caked soldiers; the stupid, yellow, cowardly soldiers; the pompous, authoritative corporals; the dreamy, valiant, faithful soldiers rose to their feet and stood at attention. As the tall, spare figure advanced nearer, tired hands were smartly raised to their helmets and dropped quickly against the thigh.

Was it General Ulysses S. Pershing who had come? It was not. It was Major Adams, Major John R. Adams, the battalion commander.

"What outfit is this?" The Major's tone was crisp.

"First battalion of the Sixth, sir."

"Where are the rest of the men?"

"All the men are here, sir."

"What! This is not a battalion, it's a platoon. This was a hell of a way to let a bunch of Germans treat you."

He walked past. The men sank back on the ground, fully one-fifth of the number that had attacked.

That afternoon beer was rationed by the Mess Sergeant, who had deprived his safe dugout, far in the rear, of his pleasant company for a few hours. The Mess Sergeant admitted that the beer had been provided by Major Adams.

On this particular afternoon the woods of Villers Cotterets was as quiet and peaceful as a statue of stone. Placid, motionless, the leaves of the trees looked as if they were made of wax. Their branches curved solemnly and prayerfully toward each other, meeting and forming successions of arches. Planted in perpendicular rows, they aspired straight and immutable, while overhead, fat plucked cotton tops, greatly expanded, lay like dead below an impenetrable expanse of blue sky. Upon the fragile blades of grass men were held in the vice of a sleep of exhaustion. Five miles from the woods the guns along the front line, where men waited, anxiously watching the movements of each other, were silent.

Somewhere among the solemn and still branches a huge limb cracked. It fell rapidly and with a horrific sound through the foliage. Down, down it came, rending the small sprigs of green as it fell. Below the limb a soldier slept. When it reached the earth its heavier end struck the soldier on the head, crushing his skull. Instantly, the scene was changed to one of frenzied activity. Men leaped to their feet and ran out of the woods.

The treachery, the unexpectedness of the calamity remained unshakable in the mind of Garrett. To him it seemed the height of cruelty, and in some way he interpreted it as an intentional act of the enemy. He knew better. He knew that a shell, probably the day before, during the heavy bombardment, had struck the limb and partly severed it, and afterward its great weight had brought itself down. It preyed upon him dreadfully. That anyone could have gone through the punishment of the attack unharmed and then have returned to a place of safety only to be killed was more than he could stand. It was an act of vengeance, and he believed it to be the vengeance of an angry God.

Men returned to the woods from under orders of the officers, who feared that their presence in the field might attract the attention of the enemy. Nearly all of them returned and resumed their sleep. But not Garrett. He was firmly decided against the woods. He would be at hand for as many attacks as General Headquarters could devise; he would do his part in advancing the Allied cause; he would help save the world for democracy; he would make war to end war; he would tolerate Y.M.C.A. secretaries; he would go without food, clothing, and sleep - so he told the officers - but he would not return to the woods. He lay down outside in the wheat, every muscle twitching. For him he felt, life had ended, the world had come to a full stop.

Even the maneuvering of a small German plane around the big French observation balloon failed to draw his attention. The little plane would draw away like some gamecock, and then dash for the balloon, spurting a stream of incendiary bullets as it flew, then draw away again and repeat the operation. At last the plane drove the observer from his post. High above the trees, he leaned from the basket and dropped, clinging to his unfolding parachute. The parachute caught in the top of one of the trees. From nowhere a low-hung French automobile, with three men in the seats, dashed forward toward the scene. The men got out, and, after a while, returned with the wounded observer, a white bandage on his arm showing distinctly for a distance. But the sight offered no titillations for Garrett.

Before dusk the battalion was formed and orders were given to march back to the line of reserve. The news that the destination of the Battalion was farther from the front was skeptically received. The men adopted the pose of feeling insulted at having been offered so poor a ruse. "Reserve, my eye. Why don't they say we're goin' to one of them rest camps you always hear so much about?"

"Or else tell us that we're goin' to get thirty days' leave each."

"Yeh, where's them boats we was goin' to see?"

"I'd like to know."

"We may go in reserve, but it'll be in reserve of the Germans."

Thus, they offered their various comments upon the foolishness of believing that they were to leave the front.

But the talk was born on weak wings. For the moment the men had little interest in their destination, save that they wanted it to be near. Their legs felt as if they were to be separated from their bodies at the groin. Their feet felt as if their shoes were full of small, sharp pebbles. Major Adams, leading his horse and walking beside the men, encouraged them, saying that they would halt in a short time.

If the Battalion as a body troubled little about where they were going, Garrett cared not at all. The incident of the falling tree had broken him. He felt in danger of his life. Where he went mattered not. There was no safety anywhere. He tramped along the road, an atom in the long, lean line, his face showing white and strained through the dirt.

As night came on and a lopsided moon appeared, the Battalion turned towards a woods, was halted, and lay down.

In the dark Garrett and Morrow found a place where the grass was thickest. They spread out their blankets and lay down. Morrow was restless, though his body was scourged with fatigue. His was the foraging spirit. There were no supply wagons in sight from which to pilfer, there were no field kitchens, with the cooks stewing a barely edible mess of tomatoes, beef-bones, potatoes, and onions. He got up and silently stole away. Less than an hour afterward he returned, his arms laden with bottles and condiments. He uncorked a bottle, placed the open end under Garrett's nose, and gently shook him.

"Oh, Garrett, Garrett, look what Daddy's got."

Garrett awakened with a start, almost knocking the bottle from Morrow's hand.

"Cognac?" Garrett greedily asked.

"Naw suh," deprecatingly, "but it's pretty good champagne."

Garrett drank, passed the bottle to Morrow. The bottle played shuttlecock between them. Suddenly, Garrett felt impelled to talk.

"Morrow, I'm all in. I feel sort of sick. I don't believe I can go up to the front anymore."

"What's the matter?" sympathetically. "These Big Berthas got you fooled?"

"No," thoughtfully. "That isn't it. I can stand that all right. I can even stand to see Phillips and the rest of those fellows get knocked off. I suppose I could even stand it to get killed myself. You don't make such a hell of a fuss when you get killed. But it seems so damned ridiculous. Take our going over the other day. A full battalion starting off and not even a fifth of them coming back. And what did they do? What did we do? We never even saw a German. They just laid up there and picked us off - direct hits with their artillery every time! That's hell . . . you know. Think of being sent out to get killed, and the person who sends you not knowing where you're going! It looks crazy. Like goin' up to the Kaiser and saying: Here, chop my head off. And I was talking to a Frog today, a Frog that gave me some coffee, and he said that this damned war might keep up for years. Now, it'd be all right if we could go up and clean things up with one big smash, but it's pretty mean when you go up and come back, go up and come back, until you get knocked off. Gimme another drink."

"And Morrow, you know that Frog I was tellin' you about? When he gave me the coffee he asked me if I was an American. I guess he thought at first that I was an Englishman, and when I told him, he looked sort of glad. Then he looked as if he expected me to agree with him and said that the Englishmen were no good."

"Well, you did, didn't you? I'd like to take a crack at them lime-juicers."

"What difference does that make? The point is, the French hate the English and the English hate the Americans and the Americans hate the Germans, and where the hell is it all goin' to end? Gimme another drink."

"I guess that fellow being killed this afternoon got on my nerves," Garrett finished.

Garrett drank until he was drunk, not sickeningly drunk, but until his brain was numbed.

Morrow sat awake, watching the stars through the trees and listening to one of the new men singing low some Italian love-song that he had learned in Rome.

The Battalion slept until noon. When they awoke, the field kitchens, drawn up not far from them, were concocting the rations into that particular delicacy known to army folks as slum. The men fell in line before the large metal containers, where soiled-looking ragamuffins slopped a pale, watery substance into the dirty mess-kits that were held out by the men as they passed. The bread was white, there was much coffee that was hot. Further than that the desires of the men did not wing.

Late afternoon found the Battalion on the road again, bound farther from the advance. They knew that they were leaving the front by the receding boom of the artillery.

They were billeted in a small town from which all of the able-bodied inhabitants had flown. Vacant houses were searched; armfuls of straw were taken from the barns and arranged in neat piles on the stone floors of the houses. By sleeping in pairs, they were able to use one blanket to put over the straw, the other blanket to cover their bodies.

There began the regular soldier's formula of reveille and morning exercises; a scrawny breakfast and a morning of drill; a heavy, lumpy lunch and an afternoon of skirmishing, alternating with lectures on the maneuvers of war; a thin, skimpy supper, leaving the men free in the evening to bribe the townspeople to sell them eggs, salads, rabbit, cognac, and wine.

Of an evening they would gather in cafes, small, snug ones, with rough boards for tables and several broken chairs, and talk over the grievances that the day had brought; of the rottenness of the Y.M.C.A., upon which all but two were agreed; of what they did before they enlisted in this man's army; of the slackness of the mail delivery; of their hatred and contempt for the military police, and especially those military police in Paris of whom horrifying tales of cruelty were told; of what they were going to do when they were released from the army; of the vengeance they were planning against at least three officers; of how they were going to circumvent being captured for the next war. One, now and again, would shyly bring a pocket-worn photograph forth and show it to those whom drink had made his closest friends. In all, a fairly pleasant existence.

But Garrett was one of the more silent among them. After the first few nights in the town he began making long, lonely pilgrimages to nearby towns and returning late after taps, at which time he was supposed to be in bed. He also began drinking more heavily, and one morning, when the whistle was blown for drill, Garrett was still drunk from the effects of the liquor of the night before. But being one of the handful of the original members of the platoon, little by way of reprimand was said.

CHAPTER TWENTY-THREE

Immensely imposing by greatness of numbers, the regiments waited in ranks on the field. Presenting a huge sight of restless attention, they swayed like the waves of a mud-colored sea. Before them an officer stood on a platform, his hat in his hand, the wind blowing his hair. Not far off, on the outskirts of a ramshackle village, old Frenchmen, their wives, and their grandchildren watched. The officer lifted his hand with a gesture, commanding a silence that none could mistake. He hunched up his shoulders and frowned disapproval; he fastened his thumbs in the strap of his belt. His protuberant belly kept him from being an exact replica of an old turkey-cock. Now, tearing to shreds the phlegm in his gullet, he opened his mouth: "Men, no doubt some of you, most of you, believe that you are here by chance. That any divisions might have been called in place of you. Men, you are not here by chance. It is because I, personally, requested our distinguished Commanding Officer that your divisions make up my army corps that you are here."

Here he paused. He was a Major-General and he was wondering how much longer the war would last, hoping that it would continue through the year.

"I have watched you enter the lines, green and unseasoned troops, at Cantigny and Chateau-Thierry, and assault the enemy with such force that you threw back his most valiant troops, the Prussian Guards. You have shown your sterling mettle at Soissons and Saint Mihiel, advancing far beyond the objective given you. Jaulny and Thiacourt and Montfaucon have fallen under your irresistible onslaught. Now you may be considered, you are considered, wherever civilization is known, as shock troops, second in valor to none."

He paused, wondering irresistibly whether his impending rise to Lieutenant-General would give his wife access into the more imposing homes of Washington.

"And so you are here, good soldiers who have done your duty and are willing to do it again. Many of you men came over to France with the belief that the war would soon be over and you would return home again to indulge in your inalienable right to life, liberty, and the pursuit of happiness."

"Hooray!" shouted the men."

"You will return home soon, but not as soon as you expected. Not until we have pierced the enemy lines and brought them to our feet. It depends upon you men right here as to how long you will stay in France. You can stay until hell freezes over or you can renew your good work and be home before you know it. Our Commanding General has said: 'Hell, Heaven, or Hoboken by Christmas,' and it is up to us to stand by him."

The General was going along famously. He felt his gift of rhetoric as never before. His eyes dimmed and a lump rose in his throat at the frenzied cheering of the men.

"You men are assembled here today to be told of the great offensive in which you will soon take part. Many of you will not return, but that is war. Some of you will come off non-commissioned officers, and, as should be the case in a democratic army, others will have a chance to be officers, made so by an act of Congress."

He believed that he was being cheered again. He continued his address for fifteen minutes longer than he intended. When he stepped from the platform to the ground there were tears in his eyes.

In making the estimates of the divisions before him, the Major-General had only spoken aloud what the men secretly believed - that they were the finest flower of chivalry, the epitome of all good soldiery qualities. But to hear themselves so praised sounded unethical, made them embarrassed. Had they been told that they were not shock troops, that they were not the best soldiers in the known world, they would have been indignant. Therefore they hid their gratitude and commendation under a torrent of mordant remarks. The long lines were formed into squads, demanding food, speculating upon the nearness of the attack, as they marched back to their respective towns where they were billeted.

Garrett had not recovered from his despondency. His stomach felt as if he had swallowed a stone every time reference was made to the attack. He had done about enough in this war, he thought, wondering vaguely whether there was no chance of escape. The thought of the sound of the guns depressed him, their monotonous tom-tom beating in memory on his skull like water dripping slowly on a stone.
Disgusting! And no letters from home, no change of scenery, no clean clothing, nothing but the hopelessness of routine, the bullying of petty officers, the prospect of the front.

He was still brooding when the platoon reached its billets in the town to which it had come from the last drive. Instead of the unsavory food steaming under a fire in the field kitchen, there was an issue of corned beef, and slabs of black bread to be eaten. The field kitchens were packed, the supply wagons were loaded.

The persevering little mules that hauled the machine-gun carts stood waiting. Orders were passed for the men to pack up their equipment and be ready to fall into line on the Company street in half an hour.

"Shake it up, you men," the officers called, walking back and forth past the buildings. "We haven't got all night." Somebody asked where the platoon was going. "To the front," an officer answered. "Make it snappy."

CHAPTER TWENTY-FOUR

For two days now the bombardment had continued, heaving over the live, huge shells that broke in the distance with a dull, sullen fury. Lightly it had begun, and with an exchange of salutes from the six-inch rifles. Then a number of batteries in the center of the sector started ferociously to bark. Along the left the heavy detonation of the exploding shells was taken up, later to be joined by the smaller pieces of artillery, which went off with mad, snapping sounds. The guns on the right brought the entire line into action.

Artillerymen, their blouses off, their sleeves rolled, sweated in torrents as they wrestled with shells, throwing them into the breeches of their guns. Each gun was fired, and as it recoiled from the charge another shell was waiting to be thrown into the breech. The officers of the gunners, their muscles tense, their lineaments screwed up so that their faces looked like white walnuts, made quick mathematical calculations, directing the shells unerringly to strike their targets. Orderlies hurried from gun-pit to gun-pit, carrying messages from a higher officer which, when delivered to the Battery Commanders and passed to the gunners, would strike or spare a hundred men, an old church, or a hospital.

Wagons and heavy motor-trucks rumbled over the roads leading to the forests where the long-range guns were hidden, bringing always more food for the black, extended throats of the guns. The batteries in the center had been drawn up in a thick woods a few miles from the present front line. There, from the height of a steady swell in the earth, they were able better to watch the effects of their pounding.

Between the inky mass of forest which concealed the guns and the jagged front line were the crumbling ruins of a village of which not a building now stood. The ruins were at the edge of the front line, which zigzagged unendingly in either direction. Barbed wire, rusted and ragged, was strung from posts before the trench. Chevaux- de-frise,[32] inspiring confidence in their ability to withstand penetration were placed at intervals wherever gaps had been blown in the barbed wire.

The space between the front line and the German listening posts was a yellowish gray. Its face was pockmarked and scabbed with tin cans, helmets, pieces of equipment. Bones, grayed in the sun and rain, were perceptible occasionally. A leather boot stuck grotesquely out of one of the unhealthy indentations in the lifeless ground. The flat chrome earth lay for several hundreds of yards and then was split by a strip of shadowy black woods.

Past the woods the barren earth continued, rising and disappearing at a distance, in a hill studded with trees.

Beyond lay mystery and a gargantuan demon who, taking whatever shape he chose, might descend with a huge funneled bag from which he might extract any number of fascinatingly varied deaths.

The night before, out of a still, starlit sky, a sudden rain had fallen. It had drenched the trees and the grass and soaked the clothing of the troops who were lying in the woods awaiting the hour for the attack. The rain made a long, slimy, muddy snake out of the roads leading to the front line. Where the caisson tracks had bitten into the ground, hasty rivulets now ran. Water from the evenly plotted fields had drained into the ditch that ran alongside the road, overflowing.

---

[32] A defensive anti-cavalry measure consisting of a portable frame (sometimes just a simple log) covered with many projecting long iron or wooden spikes or spears.

Bandoliers of ammunition slung over their shoulders, their pockets stuffed with heavy corrugated hand-grenades, carrying shovels and picks, the platoon followed along the muddy road in rear of a machine-gun company. Rudely awakened from an irresistible sleep beneath the trees, they had been marshaled before supply wagons, had been given articles of extra equipment to use in the attack. Now, whenever the body of troops before them halted, the lids closed readily over their sleepy eyes and their bodies swayed with fatigue. The halts were frequent, for the machine-gunners carried their heavy rifles and tripods on their shoulders.

The road was slippery and the travel laborious, and after innumerable pauses whenever the advancing line became clogged, the men sat down, completely fatigued, in the mud and water. Uneasiness could be felt in the tightly packed mass that waddled along the road. It lay on the tongues of the platoon, preventing them from showing their exasperation at the long delay. Curses would rise to their lips and die unuttered. A word spoken aloud, the jangling of metal, would infuriate them. From fear and habit, the explosion of a gun near them would cause them to stop, standing without a tremor. A distance of less than two miles, the platoon crawled along like an attenuated turtle. They felt that dawn would find them still on the road, their feet struggling with the clinging mud. The night was as thick and black as coal-tar. Progress seemed impossible.

Behind the barely moving lines the guns continued their boom, boom, like the sound of distant thunder. The shells whistled overhead, the report of their explosion only faintly to be heard. There was no retaliation. The enemy seemed willing to take the brunt without a murmur. But to the platoon their silence was suspicious. Accustomed to hearing the crashing reply to a bombardment, when the men did not hear it they grew fearful. They began to wonder if they were not being led into a trap. Fed too fully upon the German-spy propaganda issued by the Allied Governments, they wondered whether the General directing the attack might not be a minion of the Kaiser, leading them to their deaths. Or else, the Germans were planning some great strategic coup.

The failure of the enemy guns to reply was so annoying that it became the absorbing notion in the minds of the men. Their ears were strained, waiting to hear the familiar whine of a shell fired toward them. It made their nerves feel ragged and exposed. On the road sounded the decisive beat of horses' hoofs; it was deeply perturbing. Stretching their necks, unmindful of the slippery road, the danger of sliding into the ditch, the men watched the horse and rider, believing it portentous. The horse was turned back to the woods.

Like a latrine built for a corps of monsters stretched the slippery trench. Approaching it through the narrow communication gully, the men slid and stumbled from the slatted-board bottom into the mire. They would withdraw their legs from the mud, the mud making a pflung sound as the foot rose above it.

The platoon filed into the trench, and crouched low against the firing bays, their bayonets peeping over the top. After hours on the road the trench was warm to their bodies, despite its mud and slime. Their eyes staring into the black night, the men waited.

Hard, cold, and unfriendly dawn broke over the earth like a thin coating of ice shattering in a washbasin. In the eerie light the tangled masses of wire, the weather-beaten posts from which the wire was strung, the articles of equipment and clothing once worn by men looked unreal. The woods ahead, a grayish black, lay against the sky like a spiked wall.

Garrett, his face pressed against the muddy side of the trench, felt sick. Along the road his body had been shaken with chills. Now the muscles of his stomach were contracting, forcing him to gag. He thought of poking his soiled finger down his throat, but the thought of it was so revolting that he only gagged more violently.

Crouching there, he had no desire to leave the trench. Why should he leave it, he asked himself, and could find no reason. Possibly for an hour during his whole life he had hated the German army. Now, he only disliked them.

And for one reason: because they marched in a goose-step. He felt that for any people to march in that manner was embarrassing to the rest of humanity. Somehow it severed them from the rest of their kind. But that was little reason, he realized, to drag his weary body over a repulsive ground. He was conscious of a sensation of numbness.

"Je's, I'm sick," he groaned to the man next to him. "I don't know whether I can go over. I'm all in."

"Why don't you go back? Tell one of the officers. He'll send you back."

"Yeh. And have every one of you birds think I'm yellow? I will not. I'll be all right," he added.

The roar of the guns deepened. A heavy curtain of exploding shells lay between the platoon and the German lines. The barrage lifted and started to move.

Whistles were imperatively blown along the trench, commanding the men to rise and begin the advance. As if it were their last mortal act, the men clambered out of the trench and started to walk.

Bent over, like a feeble old man, Garrett walked abreast of the first wave. His respirator hung heavily from around his neck. He clutched at his collar, loosening it more freely to breathe. His legs were made of wood, they felt light, but hesitated to bend. His nostrils were being flattened against his face by huge, unseen thumbs. Hell, Heaven, or Hoboken by Christmas, he thought, adding probably hell for all of us.

The day brightened, and as he approached the trees they became separate identities. The trees stared at him menacingly. They embarrassed him by their scrutiny. He found himself making excuses for advancing toward them. It was exasperating that no bullets were fired from the trees. He wondered why it could be. And then he was at the woods, entering with the rest of the men, and the underbrush parted with a crackling sound. He drew back, frightened.

Because of the thickness of the underbrush and the irregularity of the setting of the trees, he veered off to a path that led through the woods. On it other men had made their way and were stealthily tramping through, their eyes darting from one side to the other.

At a place where another path crossed, an ammunition wagon stood. The bodies of four horses lay dead on the ground, their hides mutilated, pierced by pieces of flying shell. The dead horses were a squeamish sight, lying there with large reproachful eyes and slender necks that seemed to have been broken. Their stomachs were inflated as if they had eaten too much fresh clover. Garrett grew more depressed, his own stomach wanted to describe a parabola inside of him. He gagged, engaged in a spasm of retching. The woods were covered with saffron, their trunks were gaunt, and yellow splotches stuck out from the branches. The grass wore a bilious complexion. He looked down at his shoes; they too, were yellow, unfamiliar, indefinable from the color of his puttees or his mustard uniform.

He tramped on through the woods, hoping that his sickness would overpower him, cast him to the ground where he could rest.

"If only I'd get so sick I couldn't walk," he thought, "how nice it would be."

He walked on, thinking of the spot in which he would like to lie, judging with a discerning eye the softness and safety of various spots of ground. The sight of a small hollow, with breastworks of fallen trees thrown up on the dangerous side, was attractive to him. He was about to succumb, but decided against it, thinking of the awkwardness of his position in case someone should pass. And they were sure to pass, some snooping Lieutenant or orderly.

But he was supposed to be in an attack. Morrow and the rest were facing the enemy at this very moment. And here he was lagging behind! Choking with fright, he hurried out of the woods. The rest of the line had just broken through the trees and now he joined them as they marched steadily ahead.

The field over which they were advancing stretched like a gridiron for perhaps a mile, then it was lost in the thickly wooded hill that rose majestically and invincibly. God, Garrett thought, do we have to take that hill? It was inconceivable that it could be done, yet inconceivable that it would not be done. There it rose - a Gethsemane - towering in the air, austere and forbidding.

Below, four waves of men with their bayoneted rifles held at high port, advanced along the flat field toward the hill. Garrett felt weak, as if he wanted to crumple up. Machine bullets clicked like keys on the typewriter of the devil's stenographer. Rifled bullets announced their swift, fatal flights by little pings that sounded like air escaping from a rubber tire. They seemed to follow each other closely enough to make a solid sheet of metal.

Slowly the men marched, trying to maintain an even line under the rapid firing. Silently and unexpectedly a whistle blew and the long lines dropped to the ground. For the little distance they had advanced their losses were too great.

To lie down in the face of the firing was more unendurable than moving toward it. The bodies of the men felt to them more conspicuous than when they were on their feet. They tried to hug the ground, to expose as little of themselves as they could.

"What the hell are we going to do? Go to sleep here?"

"No, they're lookin' for the Angel of Mons[33] to tell us when to advance."

"This is an awful way to win a war. Are they tryin' to get us all killed?"

"Oh, one of these German spies is in command, that's all."

So ran the comments of the men, interspersed with cries for assistance from the wounded. At last the whistles blew again and the men rose to their feet, chafing, half-frightened, half-angry, under the restraint of the regulated advance. One man started ahead of the line and an officer, raising his voice above the frightful racket, yelled: "Come back here, you damned fool. Do you want to get killed by your own barrage?"

The barrage was falling short of its mark. Shells struck the fringe of the woods toward which the men already had closely advanced.

---

[33] The Angels of Mons was a popular legend about a group of angels who supposedly protected members of the British Army in the Battle of Mons at the outset of the Great War.

CHAPTER TWNETY-FIVE

An avian sailed over the field, a serene, self-satisfied dove of peace. The pilot fired a rocket when he was directly above the front line, and wheeled back. The barrage lengthened, the shells crashing into the trees. But if the barrage had delayed their progress on the field, it had hastened it in the woods. The coils of barbed wire which had been strung before the German Front-Line trench were blown to bits. Great gaps in the wire appeared all along the line. The men rushed through, fell into the trench, and scrambled out the other side. The German trench had been abandoned. The main body of their troops was withdrawn and the hill had been protected only by a heavy rear-guard.

Through the woods men were running like mad, beating small, inoffensive bushes with the butts of their rifles, and calling: "Come out of there, you damned Boche." Wherever they saw a dugout they hurled a pocketful of hand-grenades down the entrance, following them with threatening exclamations. They were the new men who had joined the platoon at the last village, at which it had been billeted.

It was a night for love, a night for beautiful women to rest their elbows on the window casement of picturesque houses and lend their ears to the serenade of their troubadours - a night to wander listlessly through unreal woods and offer words of love beneath the benediction of a round moon.

Through a long, tortuous trench which, now and again, had been partially obliterated by the explosion of a large shell, Garrett tramped. He had been sent out by the platoon commander to find the French army, whose left flank was supposed, according to orders issued before the attack, to adjoin the right of the platoon. Picking his way through the barbed wire over the rough ground, he swung along with large strides. Importantly, he adjusted the strap of his helmet more tightly about his chin.

He girded his pistol belt tighter, until his waist was wasp-like. To his leg he buckled his holster until it interfered with the circulation of his blood. He liked the feel of the pistol against his thigh. It made him feel equal to any danger. He was a Buffalo Bill, a Kit Carson, a D'Artagnan.

Progress, walking in the trench, was too dreary for his mood. He climbed out and commenced to stride along the field, his chest inflated, his chin high. He thought of the men lying along the trench, huddled together, three men under one blanket, and he felt motherly toward them. He thought of the Allied armies waiting for the war to be over, so that they might return to their homes and children, and he felt protective toward them. He thought of President Wilson, bearing the burden of the saving of civilization on his thin, scholarly shoulders, and he felt paternal toward him. Garrett, it was who had been ordered to find the French army, to link it up with the American army so that there might be no gaps in the ranks when the attack began on the morrow. He walked on and on and somehow in the dim light he lost the direction of the trench.

The blasted French army was not going to be as easy to find as he had imagined. He had now walked much farther than he had been told to walk, and still there was no sight or sound of them. A little farther on his attention became divided between the French army and the trench. If he lost the direction of the trench, how could he find the army, he thought.

Out of the stillness of the night a Maxim sputtered. Garrett started, then ran as swiftly as he could. He fell into the trench, quite breathless. Feeling forlorn, he crept along the trench, with all his native cunning.

After he had been walking he knew not how long, a form was vaguely seen to move ahead. Garrett halted. "Frangais soldat?" he questioned.

"Who the devil is that?" a voice answered.

He had returned unwittingly to his own platoon. The platoon commander, hearing the voices, came up. "Is that Garrett?" "

"Yes, sir."

"Well, where have you been? I told you to come back, if the Frogs weren't near here. They probably haven't arrived yet."

Garrett sought out Morrow and lay down beside him underneath his blanket. Their heads covered, they talked in whispers.

"Gimme a cigarette," Garrett commanded.

The cigarette, badly crumpled, was produced from one of Morrow's pockets.

"Now give me a match."

After waiting a while Morrow produced a box of matches. Then with a sigh: "Ah doan mind givin' you cigarettes, Garrett, but I hate like hell to carry 'em around for you."

Silence.

"Where ya been?"

"Oh, out tryin' to find some damned Frogs."

"When do we go over again?"

"In the morning, I guess."

Garrett, having been in touch with the Commanding Officer to the extent of carrying out an order of the Lieutenant's, was expected to know these things.

CHAPTER TWENTY-SIX

The obverse bank of the large ridge was barren of foliage. No trees reared their protecting heads, shielding the men who slipped quietly down the side; nor did there seem to be any need of shelter. In the half-light of the gray-dawn men moved without the usual accompaniment of firing from the enemy. To the silently advancing men it seemed as if there were no enemy in front of them, nothing to hinder their progress into the town that rested in delicate contours on the near bank of the hill ahead. Warily they proceeded nearer to the lines of jagged barbed wire that ran like a gantlet, one near the low point of the ridge, the other several hundreds of yards away, where the hill rose to the town. The ground, with the deep green of long, untrampled grass, was springy under the feet of the men. Their mouths tasted as if they had eaten mud. Breathless, the blunt air lay against them. From the somber purple trees on the hill, the unnatural stillness of the village, there was a portent of evil.

Carefully, as if they were dressed for inspection, the men avoided the barbs of the wire that reached out to grasp and tear their clothing. There was no hurry. Every movement was made calmly and a trifle ponderously. Under the silence, the platoon had acquired a fictitious dignity.

The last man through the tangled wire, the platoon formed in line again, moving forward. And then, in the dim light, the trees shot sparks of fire. Bullets sizzled hotly into the pen. They struck with an ugly hiss. In consternation the platoon stood for a moment, then fell to the ground. Their hearts flopped - and stood still. Inside their heads wings of mammoth windmills were revolving. Bullets spattered on, demanding, screeching for, death. The whole sound was reminiscent of ivory dice being frantically shaken in a metal box.

Garrett, by sheer straining, tried to force his body into the ground. He felt that his helmet was a magnet for the flying pieces of steel. His shoulders felt bare, the flesh undulating over his body. A bullet struck at the right of him, throwing up a puff of dust in his face. Cautiously, counting every move, he unfastened his respirator from his neck and wriggled it in front of him. He dropped his chin, letting his helmet fall from his head upon the respirator box. A group of bullets struck near his elbow. It hastened him piling his bandoliers of ammunition in front of him. Then he regretted his action. Supposing a bullet should strike the bandoliers and set off the cartridges! How many? Two hundred and twenty. And what would be left of him? He threw the bandoliers to the side. The bullets hailed, beating fiercely like an early spring storm. He crossed his arms in front of him, hiding his head and shutting his eyes. But the desire to see, to witness, was strongest, and he guardedly twisted his neck.

Around him men were whining for stretcher bearers. Plaintive and despondent, their cries reached his ears. He did not care. A dead man was a dead man. He grew sulky, restive, at their repeated cries for assistance.

"Why can't they let a fellow alone?" he thought. The enemy continued with their torrent of fire.

God, this was ticklish business, lying here like a bump on a log! Could nothing be done about it?

He crooked his neck, looking to the right, where the platoon commander lay. The platoon commander was so still that for a moment Garrett thought he was dead. Then something in his tense position informed him that he was alive.

"Why doesn't he do something? What the devil is he good for?" Garrett wondered.

Morrow was lying in a spot thoroughly without shelter. Around him the bullets spat viciously, covering him with fine dirt. Ahead of him a small hump of ground enticed him. It was small, not much bigger than the crown of a hat, but to Morrow it looked mountainous. He had watched it now seemingly for hours, afraid to move, believing that if he lay quite still the enemy would think he was dead and not fire at him. But ever the bullets came closer. He wriggled a few inches on his belly, and stopped. He tried it again. If only the machine-guns would let up for a moment he was sure that he could make it. He twisted a few more inches, working his body snakelike. Now he could almost touch the mound of dirt. He reached out his hand and grasped at the hump. The fingers of his hand had been stretched out. Now they slowly crumpled, making a weak, ineffectual fist. His arm remained outstretched. His head flattened against the earth, his body relaxing. From the left side of his head blood dripped, forming a little pool that was quickly absorbed by the dirt. Slowly his body stiffened.

Garrett had watched him, fascinated, wanting to cry out a warning, yet fearing that his effort to help would be a hindrance. He felt himself, with Morrow, striving to attain shelter behind the absurd little mound. Garrett felt that it was his hand that reached out to touch the little mound!

"Morrow!" Garrett called. "Oh, Morrow!" He was excited. "Can't you make it, Morrow?" In his consciousness the thought pounded that Morrow was dead, but he combated it. Why, Morrow can't be dead, he argued with himself. Why, he just gave me a cigarette last night! There was total unbelief of the possibility of connecting death with Morrow in his tone. Clayton Morrow dead? Damn foolishness. But he was dead, and Garrett knew it. It made him sick to think of it. That's right. It's something you can't fool yourself about.

He rose straight as any of the posts from which was strung the fatal barbed wire. He stooped over and picked up his bandolier of ammunition. He looked around at the men lying there on the ground and a sneer came over his face. Methodically, as if he were walking home, he started toward the end of the barbed-wire pen. A bullet neatly severed the fastening of his puttee. He was unmindful of the fact that it unrolled the folds of the cloth falling about his feet.

Now, along the line, other men had got to their feet. They were all in a daze, not knowing what was happening. They sensed an enemy in front of them, but they were not fully aware of his presence.

Whizzing past, the machine-gun bullets were annoying little insects. Garrett struck at his face, trying to shoo the bothering little creatures away. How damned persistent they were! He reached the strands of barbed wire which lay between him and the enemy and calmly picked out a place where the wire had been broken, and walked through. Now he had entered the fringe of the forest. Dimly he recognized a face before him to be that of a German. There was the oddly shaped helmet covering the head, the utilitarian gray of the German uniform. The face did not at all appear barbaric. It was quite youthful, the chin covered with a light down. He veered the muzzle of his rifle toward the face, and, without raising his rifle to his shoulder, pulled the trigger. The face disappeared.

Gray uniforms, with helmets like distorted flowerpots, fled through the woods, in front of the mass of men that now surged forward. Garrett followed after them, not particularly desirous of stopping them, but wanting to overtake them before they reached the crest of the hill.

Men poured into the woods, making a firm wall studded with bristling bayonets. On their faces was a crystallized emotion, presumably hate. Lying out on the ground but a short time ago they had been frozen with fear. They were hounds on a leash being tortured. The leash had snapped and the fear was vanishing in the emotion of a greater fear - the maddened fight for self-preservation. And so they scoured the woods, charging the Germans with a white fury, recklessly throwing hand-grenades in front of them.

Their cowardice made them brave men, heroes. Pushing on, they swung to the right toward the town. Through the open field they ran in little spurts, falling on their faces, rising and rushing on. From the windows of the houses and beside the walls bullets zinged past, stopping men and sending them headlong upon the ground. A small number of them rushed into the town.

Bullets flew in every direction. Men toppled down from the windows of houses. Others raced up the steps of the dwelling. Men ran through the streets, wild and tumultuous. They returned to the pavement, guarding their captives. Men poured the hate of their beings upon the town. They wept and cursed like lost souls in limbo. All of their fear, all of their anxiety, all of the restraint which had been forced on them during the morning when they lay like animals in a slaughter-house and their brains numbed with apprehension, came out in an ugly fury.

Once the Germans found that the town was invaded, that the men had broken through the woods and barbed wire, they offered a weak and empty resistance. They would readily have given themselves up to be marched in an orderly procession back to a prison camp. There was only a small section holding the town. But the men did not know this. All of the stories of German frightfulness, of German courage, of the ruthlessness of the German foot troops, made them battle on in fear.

At last two squads of worn, frightened Germans were assembled in the town square and, threats following after them, were marched back to the rear. It was pitiful to see the Germans reaching in their breast pockets and bringing forth cigars which they cherished, and offering them to their captors as an act of amelioration. Some had bars of chocolate which they readily gave and which the men readily accepted. Some of the Germans tried even to smile, their efforts proving pathetic because of their fear.

The afternoon sun threw wan rays on the distorted bodies which fear and surprise had drawn out of shape. As had been the case with life, death had not fashioned their features identically. Some wore expressions of peace, as if they were about to enjoy a long and much-needed rest; others sprawled with sagging chins, from which a stream of saliva had flown; one face grinned like an idiot's. The shadows lengthened, blanketing the unresisting bodies. The men marched out of the town, leaving it to the dead and the night.

The ground over which they were advancing looked stunted, blighted by the incessant bursting of shells, the yellow layers of gas that, now and again, had covered it. The grass was short and wiry, with bare spots of earth showing. A desultory firing was being kept up by the artillery; every now and then machine-guns would cut loose, spattering their lead through the air. But the front was comparatively quiet. In an hour at most the advancing line would have to halt. The sun already had made its retiring bow in a final burst of glory, and now dusk curtained the movements of the men.

Orderlies hurried wearily through the rough field, carrying messages which would affect the activities of the troops in the morning. Officers, indistinguishable from enlisted men, moved along, their air of command forgotten in the effort to keep spirit and flesh together. Their lineaments expressed a dumb horror, through which appeared an appreciation of the grim, comic imbecility of the whole affair. When spoken to, the men grinned awkwardly, trying to mask the horror of war with a joke.

Some of the more energetic among them attacked the hard ground with their shovels; the older and wiser men sought out shell holes large enough to protect their bodies in case of a counter-attack.

The front was still, save for a nervous tremor running through the opposing line and manifesting itself in the jerky firing of flare pistols.

Through the dull purple dusk three airplanes circled overhead, snowy angry geese. From their present altitude it was not discernible which were engaged in the assault, which the attacked. The motors, which distinguished to the experienced ear whether the airplane was German or Allied, were not to be heard. Red streaks traced a brilliant course through the sky, forming a network of crimson between the fluttering planes. The airplanes drew near each other, then darted away. They revolved in circles, each trying to rise higher, directly over the other, and pour from that point of vantage volleys of lead.

Detached, the men lying on the ground watched the spectacle, enjoying it as they would have enjoyed a Fourth of July celebration.

Without warning, the airplane that circled beneath the other two rose straight in the air. Above, it volleyed streams of bullets into the backs of the others. The pilot of one of the planes beneath seemed to lose control. Wing over wing, it fell like a piece of paper in a tempered wind. The two remaining planes raced each other out of sight.

CHAPTER TWENTY-SEVEN

Garrett had gone through the attack without an impression of it remaining with him. When the platoon was caught between the two lines of barbed wire and he had arisen, walking toward the enemy, he had been numb. At that time his act had been brought about more by a great tiredness than by any courage. He felt no heroism in him at all, only an annoyance at his having to lie there any longer. It all seemed so senseless. Then, dazed, he had followed through the woods and into the village because such action was the formula of his existence.

The sights of the dead in all of their postures of horror, the loss of those whom he had known and felt affection for, the odor of stinking canned meat and of dead bodies made alive again by the heat of the day, the infuriating explosion of artillery; the kaleidoscopic stir of light and color, had bludgeoned his senses. Now he lay, incapable of introspection or of retrospection, impervious to the demands of the dead and the living.

Somewhere in the cimmerian darkness low voices emanated from vague, mysterious forms. They talked on and on in a sort of indefinable hum. Finally, it came to Garrett that the platoon commander was searching for him.

"Garrett is over here," he heard the man next to him say. The platoon commander approached and bent down beside him.

"Garrett, we've got to have an outpost. The Captain's afraid there will be an attack. Take your gun crew out about five hundred yards and keep your eye peeled."

Garrett failed to reply.

"Garrett, did you hear what I said?"

"Yes. All right." Garrett rose and, followed by two other men, stolidly tramped off through the murk.

He strode along in the darkness, a little ahead of the others. Abruptly, an illuminating rocket was fired from somewhere in front of them. Each man stopped motionless, as the incandescent arc fell slowly to the ground.

Stepping forward, Garrett's foot encountered an empty can. It bumped over the ground cacophonously. The men behind cursed in a thorough and dispassionate manner.

For four years the earth over which they were walking had been beaten and churned by the explosions of shells and a labyrinth of trenches had been dug.

Their bodies brushed against stiff little bushes whose thin, wiry limbs grasped at their clothing like hands.

The men had reached the brink of a large cavity in the earth when another flare was fired. They jumped. The hole was wide and deep enough for them to be able to stand without their heads appearing above the bank.

"Let's sit here a while. That damned flare didn't seem to be more than a hundred yards from here."

"Yeah, le's. I don't want to git my head shot off this late in the game."

They talked on in undertones, while Garrett, silent, smiled serenely in the darkness. Suddenly, he realized that they were not the only persons in the trench. A few feet before him two other bodies, huddled together, were discernible. He had no thought of the fact that he was between both lines, and that any other persons who were also there must be enemies. He only knew that he wanted to talk to these strangers in front of him.

"It's a quiet night, isn't it?"

"Don't talk so loud," the men beside him counseled.

He shook his head, annoyed at their interruption, and began again: "What outfit do you fellows belong to?"

"Who are you talkin' to, Garrett? What's the matter with you?" his loader impatiently asked.

Garrett ignored him. "What outfit did you say you belonged to? What?" - as if they had answered indistinctly.

He rose and stood in front of them.

"I asked you a civil question. Why can't you answer me?"

Their silence infuriated him.

"Answer me, damn it." He grasped the shoulders of one of the bodies, shaking them. Beneath the clothing the flesh loosened from the body.

"Hell, you're dead," Garrett told the body disgustedly. He turned to his gun crew. "They're dead. That's why they didn't answer me. No damned good."

The loader turned to the other man.

"Le's git outa here. Garrett's nuts."

"Yeah. He gives me the creeps."

They climbed out of the trench and scurried back to their places among the platoon.

Garrett sat down across from the two bodies. His elbows on his knees, his arms folded, he lowered his head and was soon asleep. He was awakened by voices crying: "Garrett! What's wrong?"

"What are you doing out here?"

"Tryin' to git a era de geer[34] by stayin' out alone all night?"

He looked up and through the early dawn saw the faces of his own platoon. Without answering he picked up his automatic rifle which lay beside him, and joined them.

The ground over which they were advancing was flat for a long distance, then it rose in a steep hill that stood majestically in the dawn. Upon the ground many people had left their marks: a group of bones, a piece of equipment, a helmet, a rifle barrel from which the stock had rotted.

There was no hindrance to the advance of the platoon. From this point in the line which for miles was being attacked that morning, even the rear-guard had withdrawn. But the withdrawal had been made to the top of the hill, whose crest was a large plateau. Perhaps a thousand

---

[34] Crox de Guerre.

yards from the brink, where a ridge cut the flatness of the ground, the German lines had entrenched and lay waiting to be attacked.

As the platoon climbed up the hill they could hear the friendly explosion of their own barrage. It gave them strength to thread their way among the bushes on the hill, ever nearing the summit, and not knowing the sort of reception that was waiting for them.

A portly Captain, puffing like a porpoise, clambered up with them. From time to time he would stop and take from his hip pocket a brightly colored paper sack of scrap tobacco. Then, with a generous amount in the side of his mouth, he would begin again the ascent. He offered the paper bag to some of the men nearer to him, and they accepted it gratefully, but not cramming their mouths so full as he. The portly Captain also invented the fiction that he was a former brewery-wagon driver in St. Louis and that, "By God, I wished I was back on a brewery wagon again."

The men laughed obligingly but hollowly.

The platoon reached the summit. Little curls of gray smoke, looking like shadowy question-marks, rose over the plateau in the distance. Beyond was the ridge, perhaps a mile from the brink over which the men were climbing. To the right of the ridge a long, white-sided, red-topped farmhouse rested. To the left the plateau ended in another hill.

It was not long after the platoon had arrived on the level ground that machine-guns began pouring a steady stream of lead over the field. Hesitatingly, the platoon advanced. The machine-guns were pointing too high. Occasionally a bullet, probably a faulty one, struck the ground beside the slowly advancing line, but without force.

The portly Captain shifted his wad of tobacco, spat a thin stream, and ordered his platoon to halt.

"How many of you men have got shovels?"

There were half a dozen shovels and two picks.

"All right, you men with shovels. Halt right here and dig a trench as long and as deep as you can. The rest of us - Forward!"

Slowly, warily, they set forth again. Now no one spoke, not even the garrulous and confidence-breeding Captain.

The machine-guns aimed lower, but too low. Only the ricocheting bullets reached the platoon.

They advanced until they were half-way to the ridge. Then they discovered that there were Germans much nearer to them than they had supposed. From little humps on the ground rifle bullets pinged past, shaving near the ears of the men. From the hill on the left came a whining serenade of lead. Shots were being fired from every direction but from the rear. The men threw themselves upon the ground, not knowing what to do.

CHAPTER TWENTY-EIGHT

After a long wait the firing abated and the platoon started to creep forward. Instantly, their movement was met with a hail of bullets. They lay quite still, their uniforms blending with the russet of the grass, on which the sun shone with intense vigor.

Garrett, lying at the extreme left of the platoon, was engaged in corralling those words which entered his mind and placing them into two classes - words with an even number of letters, words with an uneven number of letters. He had long held the view that the evenly lettered words were preponderant.

P-l-a-t-o-o-n. Seven - that's uneven. S-e-v-e-n—that's uneven, too. U-n-e-v-e-n. Six – that's even. S-t-r-a-n-g-e. Seven, again the mystic number. M-y-s-t-i-c. Six - that's even. And n-u-m-b-e-r. Six, even too. Let's see, that's five even and four uneven. No, five uneven - he lost track of the number of unevenly lettered words he had thought of as his activity was interrupted by the ridiculous words. Oh, when I die . . . D-i-e – uneven - just bury me deep. D-e-e-p - even. Deeper, deeper, deeper where the croakers sleep. S-l-e-e-p—uneven, too, damn it. And tell all the boys that I died brave.

He broke off. Behind a bush, a few hundred yards distant, an enormous olive that was supported by legs was hiding. Bellied to the ground, Garrett started to crawl, his path describing a small arc. His automatic rifle, grasped in the middle by his right hand, interfered with his movements. His abstraction was so great that he bruised his knuckles between the rifle and the ground. The musette bag, filled with ammunition and suspended from his neck, was another annoyance. When he tried more quickly to move forward, it got in his way.

The olive joggled ever so slightly. It now seemed to be a combination of olive and turtle, with its queer hand rising above its body.

A jagged stone cut through Garrett's trousers, bringing the blood. He crawled on, railing at the hot sun.

A shell hole yawned in front of him. Like an alligator slipping into the water, his body slid down to the bottom. He was almost directly across from the olive, and now he saw that it was neither olive nor turtle, but a German with a rifle pointing through the limbs of the bushes toward his platoon. Garrett stuck the tripod of his rifle in the bank a foot from the top of the hole. He adjusted the stock to his shoulder and fired.

The German scurried from his hiding-place out into the open. Garrett fired again. The German stopped, and, with a queer, hopeless gesture, his arms flung over his head, sprawled on the ground.

Garrett crawled out of the hole, moving forward. Nearly every one of the bushes concealed a German and he anticipated a day's occupation.

Now, other members of the platoon had worked their way along the ground and near to where Garrett lay. Bullets spattered furiously all around. Garrett minded them less than the perspiration which ran down his face in little, itching rivulets. He was near enough to the bullets for them to sound like breaking violin strings, as they whizzed past.

Wasn't that another atrocious-looking helmet behind the bush to the left? He pressed the trigger, and a volley of shots heated the barrel of his automatic rifle. A bullet struck a few feet from him, kicking up a puff of dust.

He crawled on over the undulating ground. From another shell hole he poured out the last of his ammunition at the olive uniforms. Then he threw his rifle from him.

And now the platoon was scattered over the field, hiding behind bushes, behind little mounds of dirt, giving away their positions by the slight curls of smoke from their rifle barrels. Not far ahead were the German snipers, waiting calmly and patiently and firing with rare judgment. The men on both sides might have been less human than Tin Woodmen,[35] to judge from their silence.

Smoke from the artillery shells hung in gray volutes over the ridge. Puffs from the rifles curled thinly skyward, lost in the blue. The men were, to all appearances, motionless, soundless, only their rifles speaking for them.

Then, like an express-train rattling over loose ties, machine-guns broke loose from all sides. Their bullets struck the ground beside the men, covering the space where they were lying with a thick haze of dust.

The portly Captain rose and blew his whistle, commanding the men to retreat. They needed no command. Already they were dashing off like frightened rabbits, scampering away to their burrows.

Garrett watched them for a while, felt the angry hail of bullets, then rose and followed after them.

In their desperation the men with the shovels and picks had dug a trench deep enough to protect prone bodies from fire, and into it the retreating platoon fell, released from the fear which, like an angry eagle, beat its wings behind them, against their heads, in their ears,

---

[35] The Tin Woodman, better known as either the Tin Man or (incorrectly) the Tin Woodsman is a character in the fictional Land of Oz.

urging them on. The men turned, narrowed out grooves in the thrown-up dirt for their rifles to rest on.

The portly Captain walked back and forth behind them, admonishing them to quickness of action.

"Come on now. I'm a liar, or else the Dutchmen'll be over here before we know it. They've got the dope on us now."

He paced in front of them, offering advice, telling one man to dig a deeper barricade and another not to expose himself. He turned to Garrett, who was lying still, engaged in nothing.

"Are you an automatic rifleman?" he asked.

Garrett answered that he was.

"Then take your squad out a couple of hundred yards and establish an outpost. You can't tell when them devils'll come sneakin' up on us."

"Yes, sir." Garrett turned away.

His loader of the night before approached the portly Captain.

"Sir, you hadn't better send Garrett out on that outpost."

The Captain spat. "Why the devil not?"

"Because, sir, he's crazy. Last night he got to talkin' to dead men, and when they didn't answer he shook them as if he thought they was alive."

"Be off with you," the Captain replied, giving the loader no more attention.

Garrett in the lead, the three men started off toward the German lines, to halt half-way, thus to be enabled to inform the platoon if the enemy were attacking. Perhaps four hundred yards from the German lines Garrett stopped beside a mound of earth wide enough to conceal the bodies of the three men.

"You fellows lie down here. I've got to get my gun."

They looked at him agape as he strode toward the enemy's line near which lay his discarded rifle.

An ochre cannon-ball lay suspended in the soft blue sky. Efflorescent clouds, like fresh chrysanthemums, were piled high atop one another; their tips transuded with golden beams. The sky was divided into slices of faint pink, purple, and orange.

On the drab earth, beaten lifeless by carnage and corruption, drab bodies lay, oozing thin streams of bright red blood, which formed dark, mysterious little pools by their sides. Jaws were slack-dark, objectionable caverns in pallid faces. Some men still moaned, or, in a tone into which discouragement had crept, called for help.

Each body was alone, drawn apart from its companions by its separate and incommunicable misery. The bodies would remain alone until tomorrow or the day after tomorrow, when they would be furnishing a festival for the bugs which now only inquisitively inspected them.

In the still air the scrubby bushes rose stiff and unyielding, antipathetic to the prostrate bodies which were linked to them by the magic of color. The farmhouse on the gray ridge was a gay-capped sepulcher.

Garrett tramped on through the field, dimly sensing the dead, the odors, the scene. He found his rifle where he had thrown it. As he picked it up, the ridge swarmed with small gray figures, ever growing nearer. He turned and walked toward his platoon. The breath from his nostrils felt cool. He raised his chin a little. The action seemed to draw his feet from the earth. No longer did anything matter, neither the bayonets, the bullets, the barbed wire, the dead, nor the living.

The spirit of Stephen Garrett fell silent.

GAMMON IRONS

I have enjoyed sharing with you this story of a true hero. To know Stephen Garrett is to know all that is good in humanity. Although there are no longer any of these great men and women alive today from the Great War, I encourage you to read more about them – there is a cacophony of literature available.

So, who am I to write such a story? I retired from the U.S. Navy in 1994. During my time of service I became a caregiver to Stephen Garret at McGuire's Veterans Center in Richmond, Virginia. My first adventure after retiring from active duty was to explore the many cultures of the world. I traveled the globe and became interested in the many legends, fables and myths surrounding the cultures I visited. During this time, I talked with those of elder wisdom and I began writing biographies of the more adventurous from *The Greatest Generation*. I then embarked upon a second career - teaching.

I currently live in Virginia and work with disabled veterans and wounded warriors, while writing part-time.

I invite you to check out my website: https://gammonirons.weebly.com/press.html, where you can learn about other books* I have written. You may also contact me at GammonIrons@gmail.com. I look forward to hearing from you.

Gammon Irons

The Compass Book Collection
　　West of Savage
　　East of Bless
　　North of Rage
　　South of Serenity

Cardinal Points: Rice's Folly

The Young Reader's Room
    Holy Moses!
    The Other Side
    Stepping Off the Trail
    Birds Of The Marshes
    The Ramblings Of A Curmudgeon

Lest We Forget Series
    "Soldier! Oh, Soldier!"
    Brothers, All (Arriving 2019)

Made in the USA
Middletown, DE
28 March 2018